THE Governor's HANDBOOK

The complete guide to being a primary school governor

Catherine Baird • Jill Bostock • Dr Pat Brunton
Lynn Cousins • Nigel Gann • Robin Hammerton
Graham Reeves • Craig Shaw

Edited by Graham Reeves

pfp publishing limited

First published in Britain in 2002 by
pfp publishing limited
61 Gray's Inn Road
London WC1X 8TH

Editor Graham Reeves
Writers Catherine Baird, Jill Bostock, Dr Pat Brunton, Susan Cornish, Lynn Cousins, Nigel Gann, Robin Hammerton, Graham Reeves, Craig Shaw
Design Martin Harris Creative Media
Photography Corbis, Photodisc, Nicholas James

With special thanks to Oldway Primary School, Paignton, Ilsham C of E Primary School, Torquay and Collaton St Mary C of E School, Paignton

Printed and bound in the UK.

A catalogue record for this book is available from the British Library.

ISBN 1 874050 54 6

pfp orders and customer services
FREEPOST 59
Rochester ME2 4BR

Tel: 0870 241 0731 Fax: 0870 241 2765
www.pfp-publishing.com

CONTENTS

Introduction

Being a governor is an enormously important, responsible and rewarding task. It's also one that can be very time-consuming and bewildering.

The Governor's Handbook provides primary school governors with authoritative, accurate but accessible guidance in an easily readable form. It is written by people with great experience, knowledge and understanding about schools and their governing bodies. Throughout the book there is a bias to action – it's not a book ***about*** school governors but one about ***being*** a school governor. In a sense it's a 'how to' book with lots of information and advice about what you are expected to do and how to do it. We're sure you will find it tremendously useful as you go about your vital work.

The Governor's Handbook deals with the situation in English primary schools. For the most part it also applies to schools in Wales, but Scotland and Northern Ireland have their own separate and different systems. Within England there are different types of schools, each with their own arrangements for school governance. On the whole the guidance relates to community primary schools, but where there are significant differences for voluntary controlled, voluntary aided or foundation schools, these are identified in the text.

Each chapter includes checklists, templates and further information, all of which add to the practical help available to you.

The writers

Catherine Baird has had a varied teaching career and now teaches children who have mental health difficulties. She has been a governor of a primary school and is now on the governing body of a secondary school, where she has particular responsibility for special educational needs.

Jill Bostock is an education consultant and trainer, focusing on supporting governors and school staff on school improvement, action planning and monitoring and evaluation. She has been an LEA governor development coordinator and now works with a range of schools, LEAs and other public, private and voluntary sector organisations.

Dr Pat Brunton provides education consultancy and training as principal in alc associates. She has been chair of the governing bodies of a primary school and a nursery school and has provided governor training for local education authorities and the National Association of Governors and Managers.

Lynn Cousins has taught in schools across England, always with a particular interest in children with special needs. She is a former headteacher of a Beacon school and has served as a governor for many years. She now writes educational material, and is editor of *Primary Leadership* also published by pfp publishing ltd.

Nigel Gann has been a teacher and deputy headteacher and is now a consultant in education and community development. He has been a governor of a number of schools and is currently chair of the governing body of a primary school. He is widely published and broadcast and provides governor training throughout England and Wales.

Robin Hammerton is headteacher of a voluntary aided primary school. He is currently seconded to his LEA, working in an advisory role with other headteachers. Previously, he was teacher governor in two schools. He has been a member of, and presenter at, appeals panels and other committees. He is also an Ofsted inspector.

Graham Reeves is a former primary school headteacher who is now director of school management with Fieldwork Education, working with schools throughout the world. He is author of a number of books and former editor of *Primary File*. He has been an Ofsted inspector and a member of the Special Educational Needs Tribunal.

Craig Shaw has had many years' experience as a governor and chair of governing bodies for a variety of schools. He has been a member and chair of appeals panels and other local authority committees. He was an LEA governance service manager and now works as a consultant with schools and governing bodies.

The governing body

Dr Pat Brunton

The big picture

As a member of a governing body you are part of the big picture in delivering high-quality education for all children. You are one important player in a wider partnership, which also includes parents, the staff in the school, the local education authority (LEA), the foundation if appropriate, and the government. Each of these partners contributes in different ways, supported by a legal framework that sets out their roles and responsibilities. The aim of all the partners is to make sure that children acquire the knowledge and develop the skills and attitudes needed to play their full part as citizens of the future.

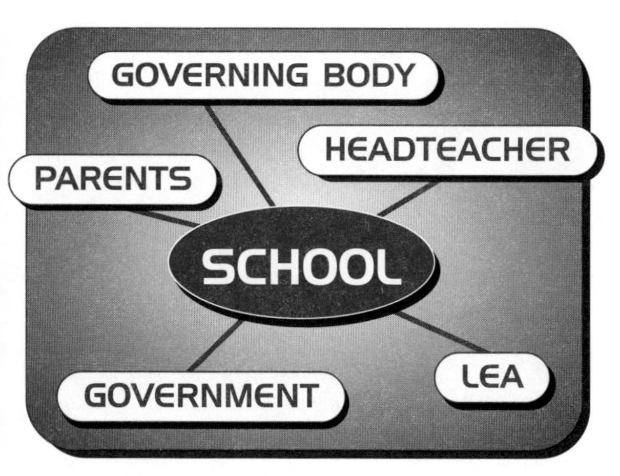

The partners

Parents are responsible for making sure that their children are educated between the ages of 5 and 16. Statutory school age begins in the term after a child's fifth birthday. The vast majority of children attend school, but some parents choose to educate their children at home. Parents of children who attend your school must make sure that they do so regularly and punctually. They sign a parental declaration as part of a home–school agreement, which sets out the school's and the parents' responsibilities.

The **headteacher** is responsible for the day-to-day management of the school. Leading the **staff** of the school, the head is responsible for providing high-quality education for all children. The head has specific responsibilities for all aspects of the management of your school, and these are detailed in the current *School Teachers Pay and Conditions Document* (DfES, 2002). In addition, your governing body may choose to delegate a range of its responsibilities to the headteacher. Often these relate to finance and staffing matters. Guidance on the relationship between the governing body and the headteacher is available in *The Role of Governing Bodies and Head Teachers* (DfEE, 2000).

The **LEA** organises educational provision on a local basis. Your LEA must provide enough school places for the children in your area. It must make sure that the quality of education is good in all schools and that it is suitable for all children. It sets broad targets for children's achievement, monitors schools' progress and provides support services. It also has responsibilities for children's welfare, for organising transport and supporting children with special educational needs (SEN). Your LEA has an education development plan, which sets out its plans for raising children's achievement in all its schools. The LEA is responsible for distributing government funding to its schools to ensure that there are adequate resources to support high-quality education. Funding is distributed according to a locally agreed formula, which is different for every area of the country. All LEAs must operate a policy of 'best value' to make sure public funds are used efficiently. Further details of the roles and responsibilities of LEAs are set out in the *Code of Practice on Local Education Authority–School Relations* (DfEE, 2001c).

If yours is a **foundation** or voluntary school there is a trust deed that influences its character and may affect some areas of its management. The school will have a particular ethos or culture which makes it distinct in some way. The foundation that established it maintains an involvement in the school through membership of the governing body and makes sure that this distinctiveness is not lost.

The **government** passes laws related to all areas of school life. This includes the legal framework within which you operate. It provides funding for the state education system to LEAs and monitors the LEA's progress with its education development plan. It determines the curriculum taught in your school, sets national targets for pupil performance and monitors school progress through Ofsted inspections.

The **governing body** is accountable to the LEA for the money that has been delegated to you to run your school. You are also responsible for the standard of education your school provides.
You have particular responsibilities relating to admissions, children's attendance and behaviour, the curriculum, SEN provision, the length of the school day and the school year, premises, staffing, finance, links with parents, complaints and inspection. This can be summed up by saying that

the conduct or overall management of the school is under the direction of the governing body.

As partners in this complex educational management system you will find that you will be most effective if you work at a strategic level. Keep focusing on the big ideas and the vision and values of the school and don't get bogged down with the details of day-to-day management, which is the responsibility of your headteacher. The information and advice you need to help you do this are contained in the remainder of this chapter and in the later sections of this book.

Are governing bodies new?

Over the past few years there has been much debate over the increasing responsibilities placed on governing bodies. Some governors welcome their changing role – others don't. It would be easy to imagine that change in the way schools are governed is a recent thing. Not so.

For over 600 years members of the local community have had an important contribution to make to the life of schools. As long ago as 1392, Winchester School had a body of trustees who were charged to visit, inspect, correct and reform. Over time community involvement spread to all publicly funded schools. Boards of managers were developed through the Education Acts of 1870, 1902 and 1944.

In 1975 the Taylor Committee (HMSO, 1975) recommended that each school should have a community-based governing body. The governing body would bring together people with a broad range of interests to help make decisions on curriculum policy, spending, appointments and discipline. These recommendations became law in the 1986 Education Act.

In 1998 the School Standards and Framework Act brought new arrangements for governing bodies. These are reviewed and updated regularly by the Secretary of State for Education and you will find that regular amendments to these regulations appear almost every year.

Future developments are likely to produce a new approach to the legislation of school governance with a shift towards giving schools greater flexibility in deciding the size and composition of their governing body to suit local circumstances, while still recognising the rights and responsibilities of the principal stakeholders.

From this very brief history it's easy to see that the idea of community involvement in schools isn't new. What changes over time is the role you are expected to play as a governor so that you can take an active part in the life of your school. As the role of the school develops, the role of the governing body changes to keep pace with it.

Are all governing bodies the same?

Not all schools (or governing bodies) are the same. There are several different types of primary school and the membership, powers and responsibilities of governing bodies vary depending on the type of school. Most of the differences are to do with how the school was established, who owns the school premises and who employs the staff.

Your school will be one of the following four types.

1 **Community and community special schools**. Most schools in the country fall into this category. The school will have been set up by the LEA at some time in the past to serve the needs of the local community. The buildings and land are owned, or occasionally leased, by the LEA. The staff of the school, both teaching and non-teaching, are all employed by the LEA.

2 **Voluntary controlled schools**. Schools in this category were established by a foundation, usually a church. They provide the same range of education as community schools but also reflect the ethos of the foundation that established them. The premises are held on trust by the foundation but the LEA employs the staff.

3 **Voluntary aided schools**. These schools were also established by a foundation, often a church. They provide the same range of education as community schools but reflect the ethos or religious nature of the foundation that established them. The governing body sets out its own admissions policy, and, because of the nature of the school, children may come from a wider area than the immediate local community. The premises of the school are held on trust by a foundation, often religious, and the governing body has additional responsibilities for the upkeep of the buildings. The governing body also employs the staff of the school, both teaching and non-teaching.

4 **Foundation or foundation special schools**. In these schools the premises are held on trust by a foundation or a specially constituted 'foundation body'. The governing body has the responsibility for employing the staff in these schools and also has responsibility for admissions.

Why be a governor?

This is a good question. Why would anyone want to take on the responsibility of being a school governor?

You may feel the following are among the challenges of the job.

- It's time consuming – you have to make time in a life that may already be very busy.
- There are hard decisions to make and you will soon become aware that you can't please all of the people all of the time.
- Meetings are never 'at the right time' and if you miss more than one meeting in a row you run the risk of being disqualified as a governor.
- There's loads of paperwork to read, to understand, to remember to bring to meetings and to store. Your local postal worker will soon see the disadvantages of you being a governor when there is yet another large brown envelope to be delivered!
- Sometimes it can keep you awake at night – the decisions you help to make affect the welfare and the lives of all the children, staff and parents of your school.

BUT... fortunately there are some very significant positives.

- Being a school governor is a privilege – you are a small but very important part in an educational system with a very long history.
- The decisions you make will have a huge impact on children's lives.
- You are creating the future, changing the present and protecting the past.
- You get the chance to work in a good team and learn many new skills as a result of this experience.
- You develop as a person and may even find that your experiences as a governor influence future career and life choices.
- You make friends and meet many people from all walks of life whom you probably would not have otherwise encountered.
- Above all, being a governor is rewarding, and it's certainly character-building!

As you might expect, these differences are reflected in the make-up of the governing bodies of each of these school types. Each has a distinct membership related to the way the school was established and the way it now operates. You will find full details in *A Guide to the Law for School Governors* (DfES, 2001a).

It's important to remember that, whatever the type of school, you as the governing body must always have high educational standards in mind when you make decisions or take action.

Throughout this book, the assumption is that you are a governor of a community primary school. However, most things that are dealt with apply to other types of school as well. Where there are significant differences these are highlighted in the text.

What sort of people are governors?

Not all governors are the same. In fact, it is very important that they are different and bring different perspectives to the governing body. On each governing body there will be people representing different groups such as parents, teachers and members of the local community. Like all schools you will have an 'instrument of government', which sets out how the governing body of your particular school is made up.

The size of your school will affect the number of governors you have. The groups represented on your governing body will depend on the type of school. Members of the governing body will have been elected, appointed or co-opted depending on the group they represent.

- **Parent governors** have at least one child at the school at the time they stand for election and are elected by the other parents who also have children at the school.
- **Teacher governors** are either full-time or part-time members of the teaching staff and are elected by their fellow teachers.
- **Staff governors** represent the non-teaching staff, full time and part time, and are elected by their fellow support staff members.
- **Appointed governors** are representatives of the LEA, the foundation or the trustees of the school and represent the views of these organisations.
- **Co-opted governors** are members of the local community who are invited to join the governing body by their fellow governors.

All governors are elected or appointed for a period of four years in the first instance. As a member of a governing body you will fall into one these groups.

Parent governors

You will normally be a parent with a child at the school and you are elected by the parents of children at the school. If you are a parent governor you have the same powers, duties and responsibilities as all other governors. You are a member of a corporate body – the governing body – and you have no powers to act either as an individual or as part of a 'parent governor group', unless the governing body has given you specific permission to do so.

As a parent governor you are in a good position to understand the point of view of your fellow parents but you are not required to carry out the wishes of the parent body, whatever these might be. You should aim to stay in close touch with and be easily available and well known to other parents. Other parents will frequently come to you to talk about issues that concern them. In these circumstances you need to be particularly aware of the systems your school has established to deal with questions or complaints from parents so that you don't inadvertently cause complications.

One area that can be particularly difficult for parent governors concerns separating your role as a parent from your role as a governor. In the first role your major concern will be the welfare of your own child. In the second role you need to aware of and act in the best interests of all the children in the school. This is not an easy situation to resolve. You need to be aware that you may sometimes have to make decisions that are not in the best interests of your own child.

Once elected as a parent governor you may complete your four-year term of membership of the governing body even if your child is no longer at the school. In some circumstances you may wish to do this, and to continue to contribute to the life of the school. However, in other circumstances you may wish to stand down and make way for another parent who has a child at the school. The important thing is that the choice is yours. If you have enjoyed your role as a governor, it may be that your fellow governors will want to keep you on the governing body in another capacity, perhaps as a co-opted governor.

Teacher governors

As a teacher at your school you are elected by your fellow teachers. You may be either a full-time or a part-time member of staff. You are a member of a corporate body – the governing body – and have the same powers, duties and responsibilities as all other governors. Unless specifically instructed by the governing body you have no individual powers to make decisions. As a teacher governor you bring to the governing body particular professional expertise and can make sure that all governors are aware of the views of teachers in the school. As an employee of the school you are not eligible to be the chair or vice-chair of the governing body or of any committee that has delegated powers.

Teacher governors can play a role in all the activities of the governing body subject to specific restrictions detailed elsewhere in this chapter. These largely relate to protecting you from being put into situations where you could be unfairly accused of gaining advantage from your position. All teachers at a school are eligible for election as a teacher governor. Carrying out this role provides a very useful insight into the management of a school and you can view this as an important professional development opportunity. You must stop being a governor if you are no longer employed at the school.

Staff governors

Members of the school support staff elect their own representatives. As a staff governor you may be either a full-time or a part-time member of staff and all types of support staff are eligible. This includes catering or grounds maintenance staff who are employed under a contract of services by the school. Staff governors have the same rights, duties and responsibilities as other governors. Like teacher governors, you are unable to be chair or vice-chair of the governing body or any committee with delegated powers. You also have to be aware of the restrictions on taking part in discussions at governors' meetings from which you could directly benefit as an employee of the school.

Acting as the support staff representative on your governing body is an important professional development training opportunity. Training is generally available on aspects of the job that may be new to you. Like teacher governors, if you are no longer working at the school you cannot continue as a governor.

LEA governors

If you are an LEA governor you will have been appointed by the LEA that is responsible for your school. In some areas of the country these are political appointments linked to political representation on the local council.

In your area it may be that all LEA governors are appointed by the political party that controls the council. Alternatively, each political party may appoint a proportion of LEA governors that reflects the proportion of elected members they have on the council. However, not all LEAs go down this political route. To be an LEA governor you do not have to be a member of the council, or indeed to have any connection to a political party at all. It may be that you live in a part of the country in which LEA representatives are drawn from members of the local community with an interest in education.

There are advantages and disadvantages to both systems. If you are an LEA governor with political connections, you are likely to have access to a range of information about local education systems and structures that will be useful to the school and to your fellow governors in their discussions. In addition, if you are an elected member of the council, you are in a good position to ensure that the needs of your school and local community are taken into account when local political decisions are made. The disadvantage, both to yourself and to the school, is that you may be removed from the governing body by the LEA if a different political party wins control of the council in a local election. If you are an LEA appointee without this political link, you are unlikely to be in this position. The disadvantage you face is that you may well have to work much harder to obtain the information you need to understand and carry out your role as the LEA's representative on the governing body. You may find your LEA sends out regular newsletters or arranges meetings or briefing sessions for its LEA governors to help you overcome this problem.

Foundation governors

As a foundation governor you will have been appointed by the foundation or foundation body – often a church – which is associated with your school. Not all schools have foundation governors, only those classified as voluntary aided, voluntary controlled or foundation schools. Foundation governors are the representatives of the organisation that historically has an association with the establishment of the school. You have the same rights, duties and responsibilities as all other members of the governing body. As a foundation governor you will have an understanding of the historical background to the school and its links with the body that founded it. You should be well placed to understand the vision of the school. As a member of the governing body you have a particular responsibility to make sure that this vision is taken into account by the governing body when reaching its decisions.

Partnership governors

You may be the governor of a foundation school or a foundation special school that doesn't have either a foundation body or trustees – for example, a former grant-maintained school. In this case you may be what is termed a *partnership governor*. Partnership governors are appointed by the governing body of the school after seeking nominations from parents or members of the local community. As a partnership governor you have the same duties, powers and responsibilities as your fellow governors.

Co-opted governors

If you are a co-opted governor you will have been neither elected onto the governing body nor appointed by a particular organisation. Instead you will have been invited to join the governing body by your fellow governors. You will probably be a member of the local community and may well be involved in business locally. Co-opted governors have the same powers, duties and responsibilities as all other governors, with one important exception. If you are a co-opted member of a governing body you are not allowed to vote on the co-option of additional members of the governing body. You are a valuable source of information about how the school interacts with the local community. In addition, of course, you may well have business, financial or legal knowledge and skills that will be very useful to your fellow governors. Many voluntary aided, voluntary controlled and foundation schools do not have co-opted governors, as this role is filled by the foundation governors of these schools.

Ex-officio governors

If you are an ex-officio member of the governing body you are entitled to be a governor of the school because of the position you hold. In many voluntary aided and voluntary controlled schools the local priest is an ex-officio governor of the school. Although you may be in an ex-officio position in relation to your local school you do not have to become a governor if you do not wish to do so. As a foundation representative you may have several schools in your area, and not be able to take up a position on every governing body. In this case another foundation governor can be appointed to take up this position in your place.

> The Education Act 2002 makes changes to the different categories of governors. Teacher and staff governors are joined in one category of 'staff governors', at least one of whom must be a teacher. Another staff governor place is reserved for the headteacher whether or not she or he wishes to occupy it. Co-opted governors become 'community governors' who will be elected by all other members of the governing body.

Headteachers are ex-officio governors of their schools and can choose whether or not to become a governor. If they decide to be a governor they are entitled to vote on any occasion when the governing body puts an issue to the vote. If they are not a governor, they do not have voting rights. Whether they choose to be a governor or not, headteachers have the right to attend all governors' meetings and committee meetings. The headteacher can't be chair or vice-chair of the governing body or of a committee.

Additional co-opted governors

If you don't fall into any of the groups mentioned above, it may be that you are an additional co-opted governor in your school. This category will be set down in the school's instrument of government. In many cases the school's instrument of government requires the governing body to co-opt additional governors such as a member of the district or parish council, or school sponsors.

Membership regulations

- You can be a governor of no more than two schools at any one time. As a governor you will be elected, appointed or co-opted to serve for four years but you can resign at any time. At the end of the four years, provided you remain eligible, you can be elected, appointed or co-opted again to serve for a further four-year period.
- There is a small group of people who can't become, or remain, governors. This includes bankrupts and people with certain criminal convictions.
- If you are a governor elected by parents, teachers or support staff, you cannot be removed from office.
- If you have been appointed as an LEA or foundation governor you can be removed by the organisation that appointed you.
- If you are a co-opted governor there are special procedures that permit your removal by your fellow governors.
- To fulfil their responsibilities adequately all governors must attend meetings regularly. If you fail to attend meetings for six months without the consent of your governing body, you cease to be governor at your school. This regulation applies to all governors except those who are ex-officio.

Full details of the regulations relating to governing body membership can be found in *A Guide to the Law for School Governors* (DfES, 2001b).

In exceptional circumstances, if a school is judged to be in serious difficulties, the LEA, foundation or Secretary of State can appoint governors as part of an overall plan to improve educational provision at a school that is not performing adequately.

What do governors do?

As member of a governing body the main things you are involved in are

- attending meetings of the full governing body (at least once, but probably twice, a term)
- making decisions – ranging from the colour of the school sweatshirt to the appointment of the headteacher
- planning for all aspects of school development and improvement – from the building maintenance programme to setting targets for children's achievement
- monitoring and evaluating previous plans to show that progress is being made
- acting as a champion for the school in the local community.

As a governor you have to work within a legal framework to carry out the duties placed upon you. Schools vary greatly in size, location and the type of community that they serve. However, the same sorts of processes underlie the management of every school – large or small, urban or rural.

To do this successfully you need to ensure that you and your fellow governors understand the workings and ethos of the school. The type of school influences what you have to do. You also have an important part to play in sharing your knowledge of the local community with the staff. In doing so you help ensure that children receive the high-quality education to which they are entitled. Being a governor gives you the opportunity to use many of the skills and experiences you have gained in life.

Your role as a member of the governing body

Firstly, remember that you are part of a team. As in any team, different members take on different roles and responsibilities. You will have been elected, appointed or co-opted onto your governing body to be a representative of a group of people. This means that you carry out your duties in a way that you feel represents the views of this group.

For example, if you are an elected parent governor you serve on the governing body as a 'representative parent', and not as the parents' delegate or representative. While you would want to be aware of the views of the parents in general, you are not expected to seek their approval for your actions. Be aware that sometimes the decisions made by the governing body may not be popular with everybody. The same applies to the teacher and staff governors, who are also elected members of the governing body.

If you are appointed as a representative of an organisation or body, such as the LEA or foundation, your position is slightly different. You need to make sure you are aware of the views of your organisation on particular matters. It is then your job to pass on these official views to your fellow governors. Then, like all governors, you are there to make decisions that promote the best interests of all the children in the school.

Appointed and elected governors have a responsibility to report back to the organisations or groups that appointed or elected them. They may do this in a number of ways – possibly through written or oral reports at meetings of these organisations or through newsletters or articles. Remember the crucial issue of confidentiality, but do try to make parents and staff in your school aware of when governors' meetings are to be held, the general areas to be covered, and the fact that the minutes of these meetings are public documents that they might like to read.

Being a governor gives you the opportunity to use many of the skills and experiences you have already gained in life

Declaring an interest

As a governor you are entitled to have your views heard, and you are expected to listen to the views of others. Normally everyone can participate in a discussion. However, there will be times when it is not appropriate for individual governors to take part in decision-making on certain issues. This situation arises when you, or your immediate family, could stand to gain in some way from a particular course of action. For instance, you may gain financially from a contract being awarded.

To avoid any misunderstandings your governing body should keep an up-to-date register of governors' interests. You should register any interests you have. If during a meeting an item comes up for discussion from which you stand to gain, you should declare your interest and withdraw from the meeting entirely for the discussion of that item.

Teacher and staff governors are entitled to play a full part in the work of the governing body but are more likely to be affected by the regulations regarding declaration of interest because these can often relate to staff appointments and promotions within the school.

Making decisions

Whenever the governing body makes decisions and acts upon them, it does so as a *corporate body*. This means that separate members do not have any individual powers. They fulfil their duties by meeting together, discussing issues for consideration and then coming to an agreement about what course of action to take. Agreement on this course of action may have been arrived at by consensus because everyone agrees it is the right thing to do, or it may have been put to a vote. Even if you, as an individual governor, voted against a particular decision, once this is agreed by the majority of governors you are required to abide by it and defend it publicly.

It's easy to see how important it is for governing bodies to have the correct membership, to work by formally agreed rules and to have accurate written records of decisions that have been made. It's only when everyone knows and understands the rules that they can all carry out their duties successfully.

Everyone on the governing body has something unique to contribute and it is important to value and make full use of this diversity

What makes a good governing body?

Since 1993 Ofsted has inspected all maintained schools in England, most of them more than once, and has built up a picture of the key features of effective governing bodies. In their report (Ofsted, 2001) they highlight the following characteristics of effective governing bodies.

- Governors are clear about the aims of the school and the values they wish to promote.
- The governing body, and all its committees, have clear terms of reference and an inter-related programme of meetings.
- Governors bring a wide range of expertise and experience, and attend meetings regularly.
- The chair of governors gives a clear lead.
- Meetings are chaired well and efficiently clerked.
- There is a clear school plan, understood by all, which focuses on improving the school.
- Relationships between the governors and the staff are open and honest.
- Governors' training is linked to the school's priorities, and the needs of individual governors.
- Individual governors are clear about their role.
- The school's documentation is systematically reviewed.
- Governors have rigorous systems for monitoring and evaluating the school's work.

Working as a team

Your governing body will work well if you are a team of people with different backgrounds, skills and experience. Everyone on the governing body has something unique to contribute and it is important to value and make full use of this diversity.

To work effectively, members of your governing body need to respect and trust one another. It would be very unusual if you always agreed on everything. It is therefore very important to create an atmosphere in which everyone can say what they want to say and can discuss matters openly and fully. When decisions are reached you will all feel more comfortable in sticking to them if all options have been fully considered. For all sorts of reasons the contribution made by different members of your governing body will be unequal. Some may have more time to give, others will have special skills and experience, but less time. However, everyone's contribution is valuable and should be recognised.

The most effective way of building up a good team approach is on the job, ideally with the support of a good team leader. The role of the chair in leading the governing body team will be looked at in more detail later in this chapter. As an individual governor you can make an important contribution by recognising your role in the team and supporting your fellow governors in theirs.

Understanding your responsibilities

To do your job well, you need to understand what your responsibilities are. The first thing to remember is that there are two types of responsibility for governors – corporate responsibility and delegated responsibility.

As a member of the team, you contribute to the decisions made by the governing body and the actions put in place to carry out these decisions. This is the meaning of the term *corporate responsibility*.

In some cases, so that the governing body can carry out its duties efficiently, certain decisions can be delegated to a committee of governors, or to an individual governor. They then act on behalf of the whole governing body. This is the meaning of the term delegated powers, or *delegated responsibility*. Only certain of your responsibilities can be delegated in this way and there are some decisions that have to be made by the whole governing body. These are looked at in more detail later in this chapter.

Very occasionally it may be necessary for either your chair or your vice-chair to act on behalf of the rest of the governors if a decision has to be made quickly. This is an unusual occurrence and only applies to that which really can't be left to either the next full meeting or to a specially called meeting. If this happens it's very important that the chair brings the matter back to the whole governing body at the earliest opportunity.

Because of the legal status of the governing body – known as its *incorporation* – you have no personal financial liability for any action of the governing body. This applies provided you have acted within the law and have sought and considered any necessary advice. It is therefore a good idea to have a firm understanding of your responsibilities and to know where to go for reliable advice. You can get advice and information about your responsibilities from a number of sources including your headteacher, your LEA, government websites, national and local governor organisations or from books like this one. To help you with this, a list of useful links and information sources is included at the end of this chapter. You should make a point of finding out about

- your responsibilities in relation to monitoring children's performance and school improvement
- the range of policies that your school has, and how these are applied
- the governing body's responsibilities for financial decisions
- your responsibilities in relation to the staff of the school.

Helping new governors

In any governing body new people will regularly be joining the team as new appointments and elections are made. Because your responsibilities as a governing body are so wide-ranging, you will want to make sure that these new members quickly become part of the established team. To help this happen it is a good idea to set up an induction system that makes sure that new recruits have all the information and support they need to do their job properly from the beginning.

You could include the following items in your induction system.

- A welcome telephone call from the chair, giving information about the time and date of the next meeting and the contact point for further information.
- The opportunity to meet the head and to visit the school during the working day to meet the staff.
- The offer of a mentor. This would be an experienced member of the governing body who would help the new governor in the early stages.
- An introduction of the new governor at the first formal meeting and support from the chair to help a new governor participate in the business of the meeting.
- Introductory information about the school and the workings of the governing body.

New governors should be supported and encouraged to play as full a part as they are able in the work of your governing body. You should help them gain as much information as possible in advance of their first formal governors' meeting.

Don't forget that the arrival of a new member on the governing body is a good opportunity to re-assess your committee and group membership and review your working practices.

See the checklist, 'Information for new governors'.

When you are a new governor

If you are a new governor, don't be afraid to ask questions. You need access to information to help you understand the background to the school and the working practices of the governing body. The checklist will help you to know what to ask for. It is particularly important to remember that formal governors' meetings are not the only times when you can ask questions and gain information. Talk to the head, the chair of governors and your fellow governors.

Be aware of the information you have been given. Even if you don't have time to read it all, you need to know the areas it covers so you will know where to find information to answer your questions in the future. As well as the information produced by the school you will be given a number of legal documents and other information by the LEA. This will help you to see how your school fits into the bigger picture both locally and nationally.

It's often a good idea to make a formal visit to the school, as a visiting governor, fairly early on. You may feel happy to do this alone, or accompanied by your mentor. First impressions count on all sides

Information for new governors – checklist

This checklist will help make sure that you include in your induction pack all the information about your school that a new governor might need.

- ❑ The names and contact details of the other members of the governing body.
- ❑ The contact details of the clerk to the governing body.
- ❑ Your school prospectus.
- ❑ Your last annual report to parents.
- ❑ A calendar of meeting dates for the coming year.
- ❑ The minutes of your last three governing body meetings.
- ❑ Details of the working practices and procedures of your governing body .
- ❑ The membership of committees and working parties.
- ❑ A copy of *A Guide to the Law for School Governors*.
- ❑ The instrument of government for your school.
- ❑ The latest versions of your school development and improvement plans.
- ❑ Your most recent Ofsted report and action plan.
- ❑ Information on where to access school policies.
- ❑ Details of training opportunities available to governors.
- ❑ Contact details of local and national governor support organisations.

As a new governor on an established governing body you may at first feel a little overwhelmed. Try not to be. New governors play a vital role in introducing new ideas and new ways of thinking into established systems. Sometimes governing bodies get bogged down with particular problems to which they can't find a solution. It's surprising how often it is in reviewing these areas for the benefit of a new member that the answers are found.

If you are thinking about becoming a governor, or if you are talking with someone about them becoming a governor, you might find it useful to look at the feature 'Why be a governor?' on the next page.

Making a school visit

Visiting your school is the best way to learn more about how it functions, meet the children and staff who work there and gain a first-hand impression of your school in its broadest sense. It's a very good idea to draw up a general policy for governors' visits so that everyone in the school is clear about their purpose. Remember that when you make an official visit to your school you are there as a governor, not in any other capacity, and you are there to observe and not to inspect. You will find it helpful to have a specific purpose to your visit, either in relation to a responsibility you have on the governing body, or as a part of your role in monitoring some aspect of the school's development.

You will report back after your visit to the next meeting of the governing body. Your report gives your fellow governors an extra insight into how well they are fulfilling their obligations in relation to the overseeing of the school. As with all other papers, your report should be circulated to your fellow governors in advance of the meeting. Showing a draft to the headteacher before it is circulated avoids any misunderstandings based on inaccurate information.

About school visits

(The following guidance was written by Susan Cornish, Governor Services Manager, London Borough of Bromley.)

The governing body has a duty to oversee the direction and policies of the school, to monitor its standards and to be held to account for its conduct and performance. As an individual governor you attend many governors' meetings and occasional school events such as concerts, sports days and open evenings. And you certainly read a great many reports. None of these activities can replace the visits you make during the school day on behalf of the governing body.

and if this your first opportunity to meet children, staff and possibly parents, remember the importance of that first impression. Before you make a visit find out what the normal procedures are for governors at your school and try to read some background information so you are clear about the basis on which you are visiting.

A vital thing to remember is the importance of confidentiality. To be effective as a governor you need to have access to a range of information on many aspects of the school. Your fellow governors need to know that they can trust you to use this information wisely.

You visit school

- to learn so that you can increase the governing body's first-hand knowledge base, informing strategic decision-making
- to keep under review the way in which the school is operating
- to experience the impact and progress of the implementation of the school improvement plan and other policies
- to demonstrate to staff that the governing body takes its responsibilities seriously
- to establish and develop good relationships with staff who are particularly linked with your individual area of responsibility, eg. literacy, numeracy, special needs or health and safety
- to see, in context, some of the monitoring systems employed by the school
- to demonstrate that the governing body is contributing to the school's self-evaluation process
- to show support and encouragement to staff and children.

Your visit should generally relate to the priorities determined by the school improvement plan. If the school has recently had an Ofsted inspection, the governors' action plan will suggest areas of school life to monitor. Sometimes government or LEA initiatives may prompt a visit.

You might want to focus on

- particular subjects, key stages or classes
- the use made of the buildings and site
- the condition and maintenance of the premises
- special educational needs
- the impact of the religious characteristic in a church school
- literacy and numeracy teaching
- the effect of children's home background
- lunch and break times
- the use and condition of resources, eg. furniture or ICT equipment
- deployment of support staff, eg. caretaker, office staff, classroom assistants
- the impact on the school of reduced class sizes in Key Stage 1 or some other change in the size of the school
- the new nursery arrangements.

This list is by no means exhaustive or exclusive. The headteacher and staff may well suggest other areas where they would value governors' contributions and partnership.

Preparing for a visit

The first thing to do is to confirm the purpose of the visit with the headteacher.

Agree the most appropriate date and time for the visit and ask if there is any suitable reading to do beforehand. It may be helpful to refresh your memory about the relevant part of the school improvement plan and remind yourself of any relevant school policies. If you'll be visiting a specific lesson it might be possible for you to see a copy of the lesson plan beforehand.

Try also to sort out any organisational matters such as where you should sit and whether it will be appropriate to talk to the children.

During the visit

If the visit has been properly arranged, the school office will be expecting you on time and will probably provide you with a visitor's badge. Stick to the agreed programme because, welcome though you will be, such visits do cause a degree of disruption and it is not reasonable to expect a busy school to change its normal timetable any more than is necessary. Try to avoid excessive note-taking – this can appear threatening and will certainly make your visit look like an inspection, which will do nothing to enhance relationships.

Remember that you are making this visit on behalf of the governing body and not in a personal capacity. It isn't appropriate to make either judgements or promises on behalf of the governors. Think twice before agreeing to take a matter up at a governors' meeting. Be sure that it isn't an issue with which the headteacher should deal as part of the day-to-day management of the school. Similarly, teachers should realise that governors are not able to address everyday matters that would normally be sorted out as a matter of good line-management.

If you see something that gives you real concern, and the teacher involved cannot explain the matter to your satisfaction, seek an opportunity to ask the headteacher for clarification. Never forget that everybody has the occasional 'off day' and that whatever you see on a single visit is inevitably a 'snapshot' of school life.

Visiting a classroom

It helps if, before you see a lesson, you have been briefed on its focus and have had an opportunity to see the lesson plan. This won't always be possible, though.

Take part in the lesson with interest and do be prepared to join in with the activity – talking to children where appropriate, tying shoelaces and listening to reading. Most primary school classes are well used to other adults coming and going. Expect the teacher to introduce you to the class and explain that you are making a governor's visit.

During the lesson you might want to consider such questions as these.

- Do the children appear to be 'on task' and well motivated?
- Are all the children engaged with the lesson, or do the more able or less able find it less absorbing?
- Is there a perceptible difference in the behaviour of boys and girls?
- Are any classroom assistants well occupied?

Try to find an opportunity at the end of the lesson to ask children what they have learned – although this won't always be possible because of the constraints of the timetable.

If possible, try to have a short discussion with the teacher after the lesson. This will be the time to ask about anything you didn't understand. Finding the time can be difficult to manage unless the initial visit plan has built in time for this to happen.

Never expect the teacher to take time during the lesson to have a discussion with you.

Reporting on your visit

Your experiences during your visit must remain confidential. However, you visit the school on behalf of the governing body, so it's quite proper to report back on what you have done and found out.

If the visit had a very clear purpose, it won't be difficult to write a short summary of what you learned during the visit and the overall impression that was made. Some schools have devised very useful one-page proforma outlines to help their governors to keep focused. In any event, write honestly in your capacity as a 'lay' governor. Don't try to sound like an inspector!

It is polite to show a draft to the headteacher and to any member of staff with whom you had dealings. They can check for accuracy and clarity.

Usually it would be appropriate to submit the report to the next meeting of the relevant committee. This is the forum that normally adopts the role of the supportive and critical friend. The more effective governing bodies schedule the dates for committee meetings to relate to review dates in the school improvement plan. Indeed, in the most effective governing bodies, the dates of the most significant governor visits are also written

into this plan. Such visit schedules and reports will contribute to sound evidence that the governors take their monitoring role very seriously.

The reports will form part of the minutes of governors' committee meetings, so they are technically open to scrutiny by anyone wishing to see them. Remember not to include the names of children or staff if these would normally be treated as confidential under the terms of the Education (School Government) Regulations 1998.

Which hat?

This discussion has concentrated on the visit made to a school by a governor in a formal capacity acting as a representative of the governing body. There are, of course, many other occasions when you will go into school for a different reason, for example

- the chair making a regular visit to see the headteacher
- to lend a helping hand with school event
- to get information from the office relating to a committee meeting
- to help in class
- to speak to a teacher in relation to your own child or attend a parents' evening
- to attend a school function or educational visit
- to visit in relation to your position as a councillor or as the local priest or minister.

You will no doubt think of many other occasions when you may be in the school. It's vital that everyone is very clear about the capacity in which you are there. You and everyone else should know which hat you are wearing. Never confuse the roles or misuse information acquired while wearing one of your other hats.

Whatever the nature of your visit to school, ask yourself the following questions.

- Has the visit enhanced relationships?
- Have I learned more about the school?
- Have I helped the governing body fulfil its duties?

Who does what?

All governors are entitled to an equal say and an equal opportunity to serve on any of the governing body's committees. However, to ensure that a governing body works efficiently and effectively, it is important for some people to take certain clear roles. These roles are outlined below.

Note that there is an important exception to this. Governors who are members of staff at the school cannot hold the position of chair or vice-chair of the governing body, or of any of the committees with delegated powers.

The chair

As your governing body is collectively responsible for what it does, it must work as a group, but one member takes a leading role. The chair leads meetings, coordinates the activities of the governing body, acts as its public representative and makes sure that it is effective in carrying out its duties.

The chair is elected annually by all governors and will be someone who has the confidence of the governing body to lead the team in the best interests of the school. If you want to be chair or vice-chair you need to put your name forward for consideration at the appropriate meeting. This is generally the first meeting of the autumn term. If more than one person stands for election, a secret ballot is held – from which you must withdraw if you are a candidate. You may find that chairing a committee of the governing body can be a useful preparation for taking on this role.

To be an effective chair you need to

- have a clear vision for the school that is shared by the governing body and the staff, particularly the headteacher
- have a good understanding of the school and its place in the local community
- be able to speak on behalf of the governing body and represent its views fairly and accurately
- be impartial and maintain a balance between giving a lead and ensuring all views are heard
- manage meetings well to ensure fair decisions are reached
- act as the crucial link between the head and the governing body
- keep an overview of the activities of the governing body and delegate to other members of the governing body where appropriate.

The vice-chair

The vice-chair of governors is there to support the chair, share some of the workload and stand in if the chair cannot attend. The vice-chair is elected by the governing body every year at the same time as the chair. If you are a vice-chair of governors you may find that you are chair of one or more of the committees that the governing body has agreed to set up. This is useful as it keeps you in close touch with important activities in the school and gives you a chance to develop the skills you need to chair a full governors' meeting should you ever need to do so. As vice-chair you need to be aware of the outline of all the major issues that the chair is dealing with, as you never know when you might need to take over the chair's role, possibly at very short notice.

To be an effective vice-chair you need to

- be keen to build your knowledge and skills, and be able to set the time aside to do this
- be available, possibly at very short notice
- have experience of chairing committee meetings
- develop a relationship of trust with the chair and be able to take on the role of 'critical friend'
- act as a link between the chair and the remainder of the governing body.

A committee chair

Committees take on the responsibilities delegated to them by the full governing body. As a committee chair you will probably have experience and expertise in the area covered by the committee. Committees have to work within the same legal framework as the full governing body so that their decisions are correctly arrived at and recorded. However, as a committee chair you may not always have the services of the clerk to the full governing body. It is therefore essential that you have a good understanding of committee procedures and of the importance of recording decisions clearly and accurately.

The clerk

The clerk might be a member of a centralised local authority clerking and school support service, a member of the administrative staff of the school or an individual from the local community with experience and understanding of education structures and procedures. As a member of the governing body, you cannot be its clerk.

The clerk's role is a very important one because governors can only exercise their power as a corporate body where everyone discusses and then agrees a course of action. It is true that some functions of the governing body can be delegated to individual governors, or to a small group of the governing body, but even then only after this course of action has been agreed by the governing body as a whole. It's very important to be clear about the decisions that are made at governors' meetings and to make sure that this information is recorded accurately for future reference.

Every main meeting of the governing body must therefore be attended by a clerk. The clerk is accountable to the governing body and can perform a range of duties depending on experience and whatever has been local practice in your area.

On behalf of the governing body, the clerk must

- make sure that all governors have at least seven days' written notice of forthcoming governors' meetings
- send out the agenda for these meetings, usually accompanied by additional papers that governors need to read in advance of the meeting
- make sure that every governors' meeting has the minimum number of governors attending to permit decisions to be made
- attend the governors' meeting and take notes to prepare a set of minutes providing an accurate record of the business of the meeting
- keep an up-to-date record of the membership of the governing body and make sure that the governors and the appropriate appointing organisations are aware when vacancies exist
- act as the non-voting chair of the governing body at the first meeting of the school year when the chair and vice-chair are elected.

The clerk may also perform a number of other duties on behalf of the governing body. The clerk may attend committee meetings and the annual parents' meeting to take minutes, may organise parent, staff and teacher governor elections, write letters on behalf of the governing body and provide advice on legal and procedural matters.

The clerk to the governors is an important part of the structure that helps the governing body to do its work effectively and efficiently. The more background experience a clerk has, the more they will be able to support you. It's important, however, not to fall into the trap of over-relying on the clerk and expecting, or indeed encouraging, them to deal with matters or influence decisions that are the responsibility of the governors themselves.

As a governing body you should be clear what you expect of your clerk, including an agreement on the number of days' work per year you want them to do for you. In turn, they need to make sure they are available to attend all the meetings you need them for in the course of a year.

It may be that you decide to use your clerk only for the full governors' meetings and some of your more complex committee meetings. You must, however, keep an accurate written record of all governors' meetings and should make sure that you have arrangements in place for this, perhaps

by using the services of a member of the administrative staff of the school. As a last resort a member of the committee can be asked to take the minutes – but be aware that it's almost impossible to take an active part in a discussion and take an accurate set of notes.

The headteacher

Your headteacher can choose whether or not to be a governor. Headteachers are responsible for the day-to-day running of the school. By law they have specific responsibilities, which are set out in the *School Teachers Pay and Conditions Document* (DfES, 2002), published every year. They are responsible for assisting the governing body in its role of drawing up, developing and making sure that the school's vision, aims, objectives and plans are carried out. Your headteacher is the professional advisor to the governing body and therefore has a right to attend all governors' meetings, including all committee meetings. As a governing body you have a general duty to ask for advice from your headteacher on all matters relating to the management of your school. In addition there are some specific areas, including the curriculum, staffing and pupil discipline, on which you are required by law to consult with the headteacher.

If you choose to do so, you may delegate some of your functions, usually those associated with finance and staffing, to the headteacher. The head is accountable to you as a governing body for the management of the school and will regularly give you both written and verbal reports to keep you informed of progress. A range of information will be provided for you in the headteacher's report, which you will receive every term before your full governing body meeting. In addition, you will receive regular reports concerning

- action to address issues raised at previous meetings of the governing body
- new initiatives, both local and national
- changes in the law
- reports made to the LEA on any aspect of the school.

Specific governor roles

Although you are involved in the whole range of responsibilities of the governing body, it may be that you wish to take on a particular role according to your interest and experience. The governing body might identify particular governors to take an interest in specific features of the school. This is an efficient way to make sure that all aspects of the governing body's responsibilities are covered. Specific responsibilities that might be covered in this way include

- health and safety
- special educational needs
- literacy
- numeracy
- early years provision.

These governors would take a particular interest in these areas of school life and report back to their fellow governors regularly. You may, of course, also be a member of particular governing body committees related to these areas and will often attend training associated with your area of interest.

Meetings, and how to get the most out of them

Calling a meeting of the governing body

Governing bodies must meet at least once a term. However, most find that they need two full governors' meetings each term. In addition there will be a number of meetings of the committees and working parties that the governors have set up. Normally the timing of these meetings is agreed in advance by the whole governing body. A meeting can also be called at any time by the chair of governors or, in the chair's absence, by the vice-chair, or following a written request from any three members of the governing body. It is the clerk's responsibility to arrange this meeting and to make sure that all governors are given as much notice as possible that it's going to take place.

Timing of the meeting

You should receive at least seven days' notice in writing of a governors' meeting. It's the responsibility of the clerk to the governors to send this information out. Very occasionally, meetings can be called at short notice to deal with very urgent items. There are special rules to deal with this, which you can find in *A Guide to the Law for School Governors* (DfES, 2001a).

There are no fixed rules about the time, day or date on which meetings should be held. They can be during the working day or in the evenings, and should be arranged to enable as many governors as possible to attend easily. Most governors will have to make personal arrangements to make sure they are able to attend the meeting, and for some people there will be times and dates that are more convenient than others. It may be a good idea for you to vary the time and the day of the week on which you meet so the same people are not inconvenienced every time. This flexibility can be particularly important when you bear in mind that governors can be disqualified if they fail to attend meetings for a period of six months. Alternatively, you might decide that sticking to a regular day and time helps everyone to plan ahead.

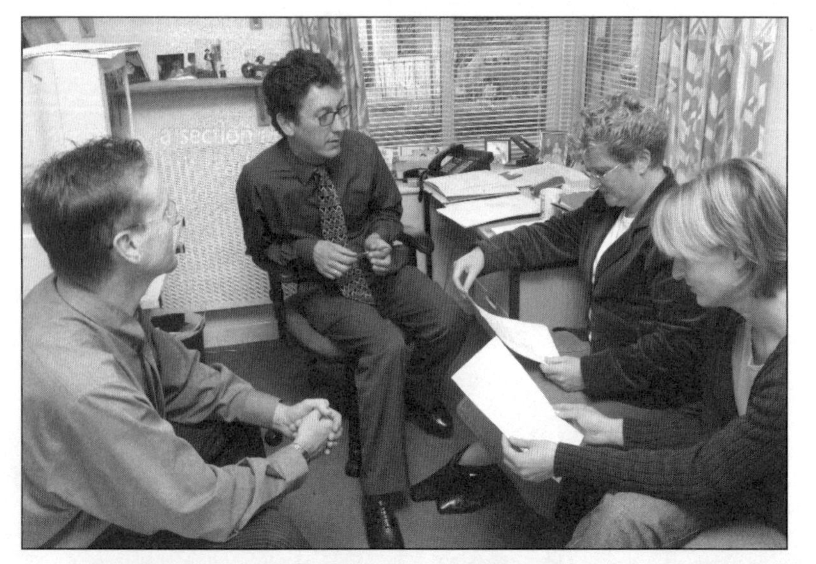

Everyone will benefit if your meeting starts on time and finishes by a previously agreed time. All the governors can then make any arrangements for attending, knowing exactly when they will be available again after the meeting. Sticking to the agreed time helps everyone and, with the help of a skilful chair, makes sure that the business of the meeting is dealt with efficiently.

It's good practice for you to agree a yearly programme of governors' meetings at the start of every academic year. If you do this you will make sure that meetings are held at the right time to deal with important issues, that all governors can plan ahead to make sure they can attend meetings, that the clerk will be available and that you will be clear about deadlines for requesting items to be included on the agenda.

Who can attend?

All eligible governors are entitled to attend a meeting of the governing body. Where you have established committees, you will have agreed their membership at a full governing body meeting and this will have been noted in the minutes of the meeting. The headteachers may attend all meetings whether or not they are a governor. The clerk to the governing body should always attend full governing body meetings. If, for any unusual reason, the clerk is unable to attend, you must make sure that someone else is given the job of taking the minutes.

When you are discussing staff appointments or dismissal, the chief education officer of your LEA has certain rights to attend, or be represented at, the meeting of the governing body in order to give advice to the governors. In addition, you will probably find that your local scheme of delegation of funding will give the chief finance officer, or a representative, the right to be present at meetings involving financial discussions – again, to give advice. As governors you are required to listen to this advice and ask questions on the basis of it, but you do not have to accept it if you can find good reasons not to.

From time to time the governing body may invite staff members to make presentations to a meeting and you may also occasionally invite officers of the LEA to provide information and advice. In some schools deputy headteachers are invited to attend governors' meetings as part of their professional development and preparation for taking on a headship themselves. Care needs to be taken to make sure that they do not interfere with the role of either the teacher or staff governors.

Setting the agenda

The agenda for a governing body meeting plays an important part in making sure that the meeting runs well and everyone gets the most out of the time and effort they put in. It's sent out before the meeting by the clerk to the governors, but what appears on the agenda is really the responsibility of all the members of the governing body.

It's good practice to agree a deadline of 10–14 days before the meeting for putting items on the agenda. Any governor has the right to submit to the clerk or the chair items that they would like to see discussed at the next meeting. Your chair, in association with the headteacher, then agrees the structure of the agenda with the clerk to include the appropriate items in order of priority. If you make use of this regular opportunity to have issues discussed at a governors' meeting, you will make sure that important matters are raised at the right time.

Some items appear on every agenda and help to give structure to the meeting. The first three items will usually be the following.

1. **Apologies for absence**. This helps to ensure that the meeting has the minimum number of governors present to continue with the meeting and make decisions. If a governor sends apologies you must decide as a governing body whether you consent to this absence, or if you simply wish to have it noted. Governors who are absent from meetings for a six-month period without the consent of the governing body lose their right to be a governor.
2. **Minutes of the previous meeting**. This is an opportunity for governors to agree that the minutes produced by the clerk are an accurate record of their last meeting. Any agreed amendments can be made, and the minutes are then signed by the chair and become the legal record.
3. **Matters arising from the minutes**. This is not an opportunity to go through the minutes of the last meeting and revisit everything. Instead it is a chance to get a brief update on matters that are not covered as agenda items in the current meeting.

At the end of the agenda there will be two further standard items.

- **Date and time of next meeting**. Ideally you will already have agreed this as part of your yearly timetable of meetings, but you need to confirm the details so that all governors are clear about the arrangements.
- **Any other business**. This item needs to be handled very carefully to make sure it doesn't ruin what may otherwise have been a very

Planning your calendar of meetings

	Autumn term	Spring term	Summer term
First half of term	Elect chair and vice chair. Review committee structure and membership. Plan meeting dates for the year. Allocate the writing of the Annual Governors' Report. Staff Pay Review report. Headteacher's report. Committee reports.	Agree draft budget plan. Agree Annual Governors' Report. Headteacher's report. Committee reports.	Finalise budget plan. Yearly Health and Safety report. Finalise arrangements for Annual Governors' Meeting. Headteacher's report. Committee reports.
Second half of term	Ongoing policy review and curriculum reports. Formulate strategy and targets for next year's School Development and Improvement Plans. Visiting governor's report.	Ongoing policy reviews and curriculum reports. Agree draft School Development and Improvement Plans. Visiting governor's report.	Review School Development Plan. Review school improvement targets and set future targets. Review attendance. Ongoing policy review and curriculum reports. Visiting governor's report.

successful meeting. 'Any other business' is not the place for any member of the governing body to bring up issues that are likely to cause disagreement, or which require the gathering of information in order to answer them properly. If an item is sufficiently important to merit discussion, it should appear on the main agenda of the meeting. 'Any other business' should be used for information items or to indicate items that should be put on the agenda for the next meeting. The chair of the governing body must decide how to deal with any other business and be firm but fair with fellow governors in sticking to this decision.

In addition you may have some regular items that you have agreed should appear on every agenda at least once a term. These might include

- headteacher's report
- visiting governor's report
- budget report
- committee reports
- governor training.

Other items on the agenda will arise from

- updates from the last meeting
- new issues that the headteacher feels need discussion or action
- items that the LEA has asked the governors to comment on
- information on new government initiatives.

Withdrawal from meetings

Occasionally items will appear on the agenda for discussion in which you will have more interest than your fellow governors. 'Interest' in this sense often refers to a situation in which you might gain financially from a decision that the governing body makes.

If this happens you need to withdraw from the meeting while the item is discussed so that you can't, at a later date, be accused of unfairly influencing any decisions that are made. It's a good idea to talk to your chair before the meeting so that they are aware of this and can advise you.

Planning a schedule of meetings

It's easy to see that an agenda can soon become over-long and could lead to a very lengthy meeting. Two full governing body meetings each term help to manage any potential overload. You may find it useful to have one meeting that deals almost entirely with the routine business so you can spend more time at the second meeting

discussing a small number of items, or possibly just one item, in much more depth.

Another useful approach is to look at the calendar of meetings you have set for the year and plan exactly when during the year you are going to discuss particular issues. This helps to spread things out and makes sure you leave sufficient time at busy periods to deal with items such as agreeing budget plans, the annual report to parents and reviewing pupil performance information.

A well-planned structure leaves everyone feeling more comfortable and able to cope and means that the urgent items that inevitably crop up are easier to deal with sensibly.

Publicising this calendar of meetings, and pinning up the agenda for the next meeting somewhere in the school where parents and staff will see it, is a good way of keeping people interested in the work of the governing body. When the time comes to recruit new governors, the more aware parents and staff are of the role of the governing body, the better.

See the table 'Planning your calendar of meetings' opposite.

The detail of the agenda

To cope with a long agenda it helps to try to estimate in advance how long each item on the agenda should take to deal with. The chair can then keep an eye on progress and will feel confident to move things on if the discussion seems to be getting bogged down.

Items on the agenda may be there for discussion or simply for information and may or may not be supported by background papers. Each item on the

Meetings – how well do we do?

Try this out as individual governors, then discuss your findings as a group. It will tell you a great deal about different people's perceptions and provide a good starting point for reviewing the way that you work.

		Never	Sometimes	Usually	Always
1	We plan meetings well in advance.				
2	We vary the times/dates of our meetings.				
3	We start our meetings on time.				
4	We finish our meetings on time.				
5	All governors contribute to the agenda.				
6	The agenda is clear and self-explanatory.				
7	All paperwork is sent out at least a week in advance.				
8	I read the paperwork before a meeting.				
9	We use the item 'Matters arising' appropriately.				
10	We have an agreed policy for 'Any other business'.				
11	We are clear about how to treat confidential items.				
12	We regularly update our register of interests.				
13	We have clear expectations of courteous behaviour.				
14	Our decisions are made clear and we all abide by them.				
15	Minutes are distributed within 10 days of the meeting.				
16	We take action as agreed in the minutes.				
17	Our committees and working parties have clear remits.				
18	We are clear about delegated responsibilities.				
19	Our meeting room is user-friendly.				
20	We make sure that funding is available to support governor involvement.				

agenda should be accompanied by sufficient information for you to have a good idea of what the item is about. This will help you to think about things in advance of the meeting, gather what information you need and make a more useful contribution when the item is raised at the meeting.

Often there is background information to accompany items listed on the agenda. If this is sent out in advance of the meeting, everyone has a chance to read it and consider it in detail. None of us is able to read, understand and pass a considered opinion on a complex issue presented to us for the first time at a meeting. Being meticulous about sending information out in advance also saves considerable time at a meeting as you can expect that all these papers will have been read in advance. The time during the meeting can then be used for discussion in order to reach decisions.

Meeting venues

There are no rules and regulations about where to hold governors' meetings. Wherever you choose to hold them, remember that full governing body meetings often last a minimum of two hours and you may be making very important decisions that affect the future of your school. The meeting room therefore needs to be large enough for everyone to have an adult-size chair, and preferably a table to put their papers on. The meeting will be led by your chair, minuted by your clerk, and advice and information will be given by your headteacher. It's often a good idea for the chair and the clerk to sit next to one another, but it helps to spread the discussion and involves more governors if the head sits somewhere else in the room. The chair needs to be able to see all the governors easily so as to be aware when anyone wants to speak. At all costs avoid any arrangement of seats that might give an impression of confrontation, or appear to indicate that any one or any group is different in any way.

Refreshments, before, during or after the meeting will help to make it a more pleasant experience, but remember the importance of starting and finishing meetings on time.

Managing the meeting

With all the other elements of a good meeting in place, there still remains the business of the meeting itself. All governors can contribute to the success of a meeting, help to make sure that time is used to maximum effect, that discussion is open and honest and that in the end the best decisions are made for the children in the school.

As a governor you have a responsibility to come to a meeting well prepared. You should have read your papers in advance and if there is anything that you aren't clear about you should ask for an explanation before the meeting. Some issues raised are bound to cause disagreement and governors may have very different opinions about what the right course of action should be. Remember that your point is best made by being polite and courteous at all times. Be prepared to listen as well as to talk. If there is something you don't understand, or somebody uses words or terms that you are unfamiliar with, don't be afraid to ask. The chances are some of your fellow governors won't understand either and will be very grateful to you for asking for an explanation. Remember

that new governors will know less about the school than you do and it can be very difficult for them, and indeed for your clerk, if you assume that everyone knows in detail who and what you are talking about. This is especially the case if you only refer to people by their first name.

Your chair of governors has the difficult job of making sure that everyone has a chance to express an opinion, that nobody is allowed to dominate the discussion and that time is not wasted by repeating the same points. The chair will also have one eye on how long the discussion is taking and how well the meeting is keeping to time. The chair will need to decide when the time has come to draw a discussion to a close. The group as a whole will often then need to make a decision on what you are going to do next.

It's helpful if the chair gives a very brief summary of the opinions that have been stated and then proposes a course of action. You may or may not wish to vote on this and come to a decision. The chair should ask the clerk to read out what they intend to write in the minutes.
You will then have a final opportunity to make sure that this is an accurate summary of your discussion and that your decision is clear to everyone. Remember that as a member of a corporate body you are required to abide by this decision even if it goes against your own opinion.

The record of the meeting

The minutes taken by your clerk represent the formal record of your meeting. Until they have been agreed by you as governors and signed by the chair at the next governors' meeting, they remain a draft record. This means that there may still be one or two small points that need to be corrected. Once signed they become the formal record of your meeting. When writing up the minutes it's a good idea to ask the clerk to indicate clearly who has agreed to do what before the next meeting. If the draft minutes are distributed soon after the meeting, ideally within 10 days, these action points will remind you what you have agreed to do while there is still plenty of time to get on with it.

Making the minutes of the governors' meeting available within the school is a good way to keep other members of the school community in touch with the activities of the governing body. Remember not to publicise any confidential items. Printing these on a separate sheet of paper that is a different colour will help to avoid any mistakes.

The clerk is responsible for keeping an accurate record of all the meetings of your governing body to form a complete historical record of the decisions you have made about the school and its children. A copy of the minutes should also be sent to your LEA for its files.

See the table 'Meetings – how well do we do?' on page 24.

Confidentiality

As a governor you will receive a great deal of information that must be regarded as confidential. This will include information about individual children, members of staff and local families. It is essential that you respect the confidentiality of this information and do not share it with anyone else. You should never discuss with anyone else items that have been agreed as confidential in governors' meetings. During the course of meetings your fellow governors must feel comfortable to express honest opinions on matters being discussed knowing that this information will not be revealed outside the meeting. Even if an issue is not confidential, it may still need to be handled carefully and sensitively. Consider other people's viewpoints and stop to think before you speak. Once a decision is made, you assume corporate responsibility as a governing body, and you should never divulge how either you or one of your fellow governors voted on any issue.

Committees and working parties

Because governors have such a wide range of responsibilities you will find that it is simply not possible for all matters to be dealt with by your full governing body at your termly meetings. To make best use of everyone's time and skills you will probably want to set up a series of committees to deal with particular aspects of your work. These committees are then given delegated powers by the governing body to deal with matters on its behalf and report back regularly. How you organise the membership of these committees and decide the areas of responsibility they are going cover depends on the circumstances of your school.

You should be aware that there are some areas of your responsibility as governors that cannot be delegated and have to be dealt with by the whole governing body. Some of these issues, such as approving the budget plan and the governors' annual report to parents, come up every year and should be timetabled into your annual meetings calendar. Others will only apply if changes are proposed to the status of your school.

The decisions that your governing body is *not* allowed to delegate are

- the election of your chair or vice-chair or the removal of your chair
- the procedures of your governing body and its committees
- the delegation of your functions and the establishment of committees
- the appointment, co-option or removal of members of your governing body
- the school budget plan
- the approval of your annual report to parents
- admission arrangements for children
- the school's behaviour and discipline policy
- the times of the school day and the dates of the school term
- your home–school agreement
- your responsibilities for sex education, collective worship and the balanced representation of political issues
- the school's charging policy
- the approval of your school prospectus
- the establishment of a selection panel for the appointment of your head or deputy head
- any statutory proposals for changes to the school, including changing its category or closing it
- changes to the school's instrument of government
- passing the responsibility for the discharge of your duty as a governing body to an Education Action Forum.

As a result of the Education Act 2002, this list is likely to be reduced in the future.

In contrast, there are other areas that *must* be delegated. These relate to staff appointments, appeals and dismissals and pupil exclusions. In these instances you need to have one group of governors who deal with the business and a completely separate group available in case there is an appeal against the original decision.

Apart from these legal restrictions, as a governing body you are free to set up the best committee structure to suit your school. The chair of governors doesn't have to be the chair of every committee and the membership needs to reflect the interests and skills of individual members of your governing body. You can invite non-governors to be members of your committees if this would add to their effectiveness but you need to be clear about who does and doesn't have voting rights. It's good practice to review your committee structure and membership regularly to make sure that it is still effective and is helping you to manage the overall business of the school, but is not taking over the work of the whole governing body.

From time to time you may wish to establish working parties to deal with particular issues. Working parties often have a much wider membership than just the governors. They usually deal with specific issues, report back, and then are disbanded once their job is done.

Confidential agenda items

From time to time you will be dealing with issues that you decide are confidential. For clarity these should be listed on the agenda simply under the heading 'confidential items' with no supporting information. They will then be dealt with separately during the meeting and when the minutes are produced. If at any time you distribute information to your governors that is confidential, you must clearly indicate this on the papers so nobody is in any doubt. One possible suggestion is to photocopy confidential information onto distinctively coloured paper so nobody can be in any doubt about its status.

Working within best value

As a governor you need to be aware of 'best value' when making decisions about how money is spent in your school. This will help you to make good use of the funds you have available and will provide all the evidence you need to support your financial plans during an Ofsted inspection.

Why not consider drawing up a best-value policy and continually challenge yourselves to stick to it?

The key principles of best value

The 'four Cs' are **Challenge**
Consult
Compete
Compare

Here are some ways in which you can use the four Cs in the overseeing of your school.

How well do you do?

Challenge

- We question why we do things.
- We are open to change.
- We have high expectations of everyone.
- We set challenging targets for school improvement.
- We expect high standards of behaviour.

Consult

- We provide clear information about the school.
- We consult on major changes to, and financial decisions that will affect, the school.
- We actively seek a wide range of opinions on our work.
- We keep people informed of the results of consultation.

Compete

- We have robust financial procedures to get the best service at the best price.
- We make financial decisions in the best interests of the children and the parents.
- We monitor customer satisfaction with services, particularly those which are charged for.
- We regularly investigate alternative sources of supplies and services.

Compare

- We use a wide range of data to compare our school with others.
- We expect to perform well when compared with similar schools.
- We aim to ensure that all decisions on school spending are made with a view to cost-effectiveness.

Your performance will contribute to the best-value practices of your local authority. Governors can expect to be consulted by the LEA and to challenge and compare the services they receive. This will ensure that the LEA is competitive.

Typical examples of committees that your governing body might establish are

- curriculum
- finance
- personnel
- premises.

Committees make decisions on behalf of the full governing body and therefore have to abide by the same rules for clerking, setting meeting dates and making sure that they are *quorate* (have the required number of members present). As you need one-third of the members to attend in order for a meeting to be quorate and make legitimate decisions, it's a good idea not to have too small a committee.

Reviewing the working of your governing body

As there are so many different aspects to making sure that your governing body functions effectively, you can't assume that everything will run smoothly year after year. New governors will join, the chair and vice-chair may change and you may even appoint a new headteacher. A regular review of the working practices of the governing body will have huge benefits even though it may seem difficult to find time for this when there are so many other aspects of school life to consider during the course of the year.

Having an opportunity to consider *how* and *why* you do things, and not just *what* you do, will give you a chance to

- get to know your fellow governors better so that you can work more effectively with them
- review your priorities and make sure they are still relevant
- look at your working practices to make them as efficient as possible
- make sure induction procedures for new governors are working well
- look at the relationships you have with parents and the local community
- draw up a set of procedures that describe how you as governors intend to fulfil your duties.

So that everyone has a clear understanding of their roles and responsibilities as governors and the agreed working practices of the governing body, you may consider drawing up a governors' handbook. This would be available to everyone, and ideally would be linked to the school development plan so that all the pieces of the jigsaw fit together. It will also help you to apply 'best value' practices in the school. See the feature on 'Working within best value' on page 28.

You will probably identify your need for training either as an individual or as a whole governing body. This is an essential part of making sure that

Ofsted inspection checklist

Before the inspection

- ❑ Check the CVs of the inspection team to ensure members are appropriately qualified and experienced.
- ❑ Make sure that the appropriate information requested by the inspection team is made available to them.
- ❑ Inform parents, staff, the LEA and, if applicable, the foundation body of the date of the inspection.
- ❑ Meet with the Registered Inspector when they visit the school for the first time before the inspection.
- ❑ Organise a meeting between the Registered Inspector leading the inspection team and the parents of children enrolled at your school. (Only governors who are parents of children at the school are eligible to attend this meeting.)
- ❑ Send out a standard questionnaire to parents on behalf of the Registered Inspector, asking for their views on many aspects of the school.

During the inspection

- ❑ Be ready to meet with the Registered Inspector or any member of the inspection team.
- ❑ Use the opportunity to make sure that the team has as full an understanding of your school as possible.
- ❑ Attend the meeting with the Registered Inspector at the end of the inspection to receive the initial feedback.

After the inspection

- ❑ Thank all the staff for their efforts during the inspection.
- ❑ Receive the inspection report from the Registered Inspector. This will be produced within five weeks of the inspection.
- ❑ Arrange for all parents to be sent a summary of the report.
- ❑ Make suitable arrangements for the report to be available to the public, possibly by providing a press release.
- ❑ Within 40 working days draw up an action plan showing how you will address the major issues identified in the report.
- ❑ Send a copy of this action plan to the parents, staff, LEA and, if appropriate, the foundation body.
- ❑ Report back every year in the governors' annual report on progress in implementing your post-inspection action plan.

you can contribute effectively to your school and should always be seen as a priority.

For a more in-depth review of the workings of your governing body, you might want to employ the services of an external advisor or consultant.

Ofsted inspection

Your school will be inspected by Ofsted once every six years, unless there is a particular cause for concern. This inspection could be either a full or a short inspection. The areas covered by the inspection and the process of the inspection are all detailed in the document *Inspecting Schools: the Framework* (Ofsted, 1999a) and in the *Handbook for Inspecting Primary and Nursery Schools* (Ofsted, 1999b).

An Ofsted inspection is bound to be a stressful time for everyone involved with your school. As a governor you will want to make sure that you play your part fully in the process. You may find the Ofsted guide *Making the Most of Inspection* useful (Ofsted, 1998).

You will only get about six weeks' notice that an inspection is about to take place. If you wait until an inspection is announced and then try as governors to get your systems and structures in order, you will clearly not have enough time, and the process will add to the stress of the situation. It's far better to have an organised annual plan, including a plan for managing and reviewing your work. You can then take a very positive approach and use the time before inspection to make sure that all governors are clear about their roles and responsibilities.

The inspection team will only be in your school for a relatively short time and will only be able to gain a snapshot of what the school is like. It's part of your role to make sure they have as full an understanding as possible of how you work as a governing body, how you are involved in the decisions that guide the school, and how you monitor the progress of these decisions. Think carefully about how best to get this message across to the inspection team and, if necessary, be prepared to take a proactive stance during the inspection if you think there are important areas that they may have misunderstood.

If you work openly and cooperatively with your inspection team, the report they produce will give you an invaluable external view of your school. The report will highlight 'issues for action', which should help you to deal with some of the key challenges that your school faces. As a governing body you need to draw up an action plan to address these issues, publicise this information to

parents, and then report back to them every year on the progress of this plan. Your attitude to the inspection process, and the way in which you demonstrate this to parents, staff, children and the local community, are very important. A positive attitude will help enormously in making this a constructive event, even when there may be some difficult challenges to deal with as a result of it.

For more about Ofsted inspections, see the 'Ofsted inspection checklist' opposite.

References

DfEE (2000) *The Role of Governing Bodies and Head Teachers*. London: DfES.

DfES (2001a) *A Guide to the Law for School Governors – Community Schools (Primary)*. London: DfES.

DfES (2002) *School Teachers Pay and Conditions Document 2002*. London: DfES.

DfEE (2001c) *Code of Practice on Local Education Authorities–School Relations*. London: DfEE.

Ofsted (1998) *Making the Most of Inspection. A Guide for Schools and Governors*. London: Ofsted.

Ofsted (1999a) *Inspecting Schools: the Framework*. London: Ofsted.

Ofsted (1999b) *Handbook for Inspecting Primary and Nursery Schools*. London: TSO.

Ofsted (2001) *Making it Better*. London: Ofsted.

Taylor Report (1975) House of Commons. London: HMSO.

Sources

DfES Publications, PO Box 5050, Sherwood Park, Annesley, Nottingham NG15 ODJ. Tel: 0845 6033360. www.dfes.gov.uk

Ofsted Publications Centre, Alexandra House, 33 Kingsway, London WC2B 6SE. Tel: 020 7421 6800. www.ofsted.gov.uk

The Stationery Office, PO Box 276, London SW8 5DT. Tel: 0870 6005522

On the DfES website (www.dfes.gov.uk) there is a whole section dedicated to information for school governors. This is an invaluable source of up-to-date information, useful links and contacts and legal guidance. From this you can contact the main national governor support organisations, the NAGM (National Association of Governors and Managers) and the NGC (National Governors Council).

The website also has information on the National Curriculum and links to QCA (Qualifications and Curriculum Authority) and Ofsted.

Your local education authority will have a governor support and training programme and may have useful information on its own website.

The curriculum

Jill Bostock

Curriculum matters

What do we mean by curriculum?

The curriculum is all the learning experiences your school provides to children. The government has set out a National Curriculum, which tells schools broadly what children should be taught. Some of the subjects *must be* taught and some are recommended. However, the detail and how it should be delivered is up to each school.

It is the central function of the school to provide a wide-ranging curriculum so that children can learn well. It's therefore a vital part of your strategic role to be involved in decisions about its content and development. You need to know what is meant by 'curriculum' in your school, broadly what is provided, the principles of how it is delivered and whether it is accessible to all children whatever their background, culture, ethnicity, gender or ability.

The school curriculum involves a lot more than just teaching children the academic subjects. It's about making a whole range of learning and other experiences available to children within and beyond the school day and preparing them for the next phase of their lives.

In maintained primary schools, all children must be taught all the statutory subjects within the National Curriculum, the latest version of which came into force in September 2000, and be given access to religious education and collective worship. Schools must promote the spiritual, moral, cultural, intellectual and physical development of children as well as addressing their personal, social and health needs. Most primary schools now deliver sex and drugs education in varying degrees and all are encouraged to follow the non-statutory guidelines on the delivery of personal, social and health education (PSHE) and citizenship across the curriculum.

For more about how the curriculum and the statutory assessment procedures are organised into stages and levels, see 'How the curriculum is organised' on the next page. For more detailed information on the curriculum in general or on specific subjects, see the lists of references and useful websites at the end of this chapter.

Responsibility for the curriculum

The government provides a national framework within which schools must operate. This includes the National Curriculum, religious education and other statutory requirements such as the assessment and testing arrangements. The local education authority (LEA), the governing body and the headteacher share the responsibility for ensuring that your school complies with the framework. When your school is inspected by Ofsted, the inspectors will report on how well it is following the framework and how well delivery of the curriculum is promoting children's progress, and improving levels of achievement and personal development.

Together with the headteacher, you must make sure that the National Curriculum, its assessment procedures and other statutory regulations are carried out in full. The headteacher must consider the non-statutory curriculum guidelines such as those for PSHE and citizenship and the National Literacy and Numeracy Strategies. Headteachers must tell the governors if they decide not to follow the guidelines.

How the curriculum is organised

	Foundation Stage (Non-Statutory)	Key Stage 1	Key Stage 2	Key Stage 3	Key Stage 4
Also known as	Early Years	Infants	Juniors	Lower Secondary	Upper Secondary
Age of children	3–5	5–7	7–11	11–14	14–16
School year	Nursery Reception	Year 1 Year 2	Year 3 Year 4 Year 5 Year 6	Year 7 Year 8 Year 9	Year 10 Year 11
Assessment/Tests	Foundation Stage Profile	End of key stage teacher assessments & tests in Year 2	End of key stage teacher assessments & tests in Year 6	End of key stage teacher assessments & tests in Year 9	GCSEs in Year 11✣
Levels most pupils work within	Learning goals in six areas	1–3	2–5	3–7	6–10 (E–A*)
Expected achievement at end of key stage	N/A	Level 2	Level 4	Level 5/6	5 x Grade A*–Cs
Statutory subjects					
Maths, English & science (core subjects)		✓	✓	✓	✓
Information and communication technology (ICT), design & technology, physical education		✓	✓	✓	✓
History, geography, art & design, music		✓	✓	✓	
Modern foreign languages, citizenship				✓	✓
Sex education		(only if decided by the governing body)		✓	✓
Careers education				✓ (from Year 9)	✓

✣Some GCSEs (General Certificate of Secondary Education) are taken in Year 10.

Some Year 10 and 11 students choose to take GNVQs (General National Vocational Qualification) or NVQs (National Vocational Qualification).

RE (religious education) is compulsory from Key Stage 1 to Key Stage 4 – it is not part of the National Curriculum as what is taught is decided locally.

PSHE (personal, social and health education) is not compulsory at any stage but it is strongly recommended and probably all schools do teach it in some form.

The governing body has to agree broadly what is to be included in the whole school curriculum and decide how a balanced curriculum is going to be provided, taking account of the social and economic context of the school and the circumstances and needs of the children. This is done through the curriculum and other policies such as those for teaching and learning, homework, and marking.

Hints & Tips

Always try to offer 'support' before 'challenge' – 'I see that has worked really well in Key Stage 1, but why do you think it's not been as successful in Key Stage 2?'

The governing body has specific responsibilities for the curriculum as part of its strategic role in governing the school. You must agree certain relevant policies, decide whether or not the school should provide sex education and keep a written record of your decisions and how they should be implemented. You decide the approach to religious education and, after consulting the headteacher, approve arrangements for collective worship. (See the section on 'Other statutory and recommended provision' on page 46 for further details.)

It's important for all governors to understand the difference between 'governance' and 'management' in terms of curriculum delivery. You set the aims and principles of the curriculum, oversee the school's provision and make sure that the school is working within all the relevant laws. You have to make sure that the school's plans, policies and practice support the provision of a broad, balanced and differentiated curriculum that allows all children to learn and achieve. The headteacher manages the organisation and delivery of the curriculum on a day-to-day basis within the framework you set.

The governing body is responsible for setting and publishing targets for the achievement of children at the end of Key Stage 2. The headteacher must send results of the Foundation Stage Profile, which is carried out before children start compulsory schooling, and the end of Key Stage 1 assessments and tests to the LEA.

The headteacher can decide that the National Curriculum will temporarily not apply to an individual child or group of children or apply differently depending on circumstances. This is known as *disapplication*. If a child's parents disagree with the headteacher they can appeal to the governing body. A panel of governors must therefore hear representations from the parents and may decide to override the headteacher's decision. You also have to hear formal complaints from parents and others about the school's curriculum, according to procedures set up by the LEA.

What you need to know about plans, policies and practice

You need to be aware of the various plans, policies and procedures that have to be in place relating to the curriculum. This doesn't mean you actually have to write such documents. The headteacher and other members of staff usually do the writing and present draft documents to you for discussion, input, amendment and approval. It does mean, however, that you need to find out how actual practice reflects the policies and has an impact on children's learning. The more you understand about what's happening in your school and why, the more able and confident you will be when it comes to playing your part in formulating, monitoring and evaluating policies.

Schools must have certain documents in place by law and others are recommended. Those relating to the delivery of the curriculum are as follows.

- **Curriculum policy** (statutory) – should reflect the school's aims and values and give a broad outline of the principles that underpin the curriculum and the approach to issues such as inclusion, timetabling and cross-curricular learning.
- **School development and/or improvement plan** (recommended) – a major part of your plan is likely to be concerned with priorities for development and improvement in curriculum delivery.
- **Ofsted action plan** (statutory) – must set out how the school is going to address any key issues for improvement identified during Ofsted inspection, including those relating to the curriculum.
- **Teaching and learning policy** (recommended) – is likely to cover the school's approach to teaching methods, staff deployment, classroom organisation, the learning environment, use of resources, etc.
- **Special educational needs policy** (statutory) – must state how children with special needs and disabilities are enabled to access the curriculum.

The more you understand about what's happening in your school and why, the more able and confident you will be when it comes to playing your part in formulating, monitoring and evaluating policies

- **Sex education policy** (statutory) – if the governing body has agreed that sex education should be provided, the policy must state what it should consist of and how it will be organised.
- **Complaints against the curriculum** (statutory) – should explain parents' rights and how governors should deal with complaints.
- **Behaviour, anti-bullying, race equality policies** (statutory) – all have an impact on removing barriers to learning and ensuring that children are able to access the curriculum.
- **Staff development policy** (recommended) – should support improvements in curriculum provision and the school's particular priorities.
- **Subject and related policies** (recommended) – most schools have a policy statement for each subject of the curriculum as well as policies about areas such as health and drugs education, citizenship, marking and homework.
- **School prospectus** (statutory) – must include certain information relating to the curriculum and it is good practice to provide parents with information on the whole range of activities and opportunities available to children as well as how they can support their children's learning.

You will find more references to related policies and practice in other sections of this chapter and elsewhere in this book.

Hints & Tips

Look at real examples of children's work, eg. to see what Year 6 national test papers in maths look like that have been assessed as Level 3, 4 and 5.

How you can find out about the curriculum

It's not necessary for all governors to know everything about every aspect of the school curriculum. The workload and responsibility for raising awareness can be shared out among members of the governing body. You have probably established committees, perhaps including one that's responsible for overseeing curriculum delivery, standards of achievement and teaching and learning in general. For more about a curriculum committee, see the 'Sample curriculum committee terms of reference' on the next page.

Governor involvement in the curriculum may also be through individuals who are linked to a class or year group or named as the governors for a specific area of the curriculum such as the 'Literacy Governor'. If you have particular expertise in an area or express an interest in a specific subject, it's a good way of focusing your time and commitment to the school as a governor and allows you to form supportive working relationships with specific members of staff.

Hints & Tips

Focus on the impact of decisions and actions, not just on what has been done – 'I know we've set up the Homework Club but how many children are actually using it?'

Steps to finding out about the curriculum

1. Read the section of the school development and improvement plan, reports, policies and the school prospectus relating to the curriculum in general and your particular areas of interest.
2. Look through recent minutes of curriculum committee and full governing body meetings to see what has been discussed and decided about curriculum issues.
3. Ask other governors and members of staff what impact recent decisions made by the governing body are having on the children.
4. Find out how the quality of teaching and learning is monitored by senior managers and how feedback from, for instance, classroom observations is used by teachers to improve their practice.
5. Volunteer to be linked to a class, year group or subject area and talk to and get to know the appropriate members of staff (teaching assistants, learning support/special needs staff and lunchtime supervisors as well as teachers).
6. Ask if you can attend a curriculum committee meeting as an observer before volunteering to become a member.

Sample curriculum committee terms of reference

Title: The Curriculum (or Teaching and Learning) Committee

Membership: The committee shall consist of not less than four governors including the head or member of the senior management team with responsibility for the curriculum. The committee may make recommendations to the governing body for co-option of non-governor members and advise whether or not such members should be given a vote.

Quorum: Three governors inc. the head or senior management team member and a non-employee.

Meetings: At least once per term and more frequently if deemed necessary by the majority of members.

Chair: Non-employee to be elected by the full governing body.

Terms of reference

- To review the school's curriculum policy (and teaching and learning policy) and curriculum-related policies in line with the agreed cycle and make recommendations to the governing body for change.
- To ensure that the whole school curriculum is broad and balanced, is relevant to the needs of all children, and provides continuity and progression.
- To contribute in collaboration with the head and staff to the curriculum-related priorities and issues of the school development/improvement plan and the Ofsted action plan.
- To ensure that the National Curriculum is delivered and its assessment procedures are carried out in line with the legal framework.
- To review the policy and provision for sex education taking account of non-statutory guidance and make recommendations for change where necessary.
- To review the policy and provision for collective worship and RE in line with the locally agreed syllabus and make recommendations for change where necessary.
- To review the school's provision for PSHE and citizenship taking account of non-statutory guidance.
- To promote extra-curricular/enrichment activities.
- To receive curriculum progress reports from the head and others, an analysis of the annual PANDA report and information about non-statutory assessment and testing in order to monitor, review and evaluate the standards of achievement, seek to make continuing improvements and inform target-setting.
- To ensure that targets for pupil achievements are set and published as required by the legislation.
- To ensure that named governors for special educational needs, literacy and numeracy and others are appointed as required by the governing body and receive the necessary support and training in their roles.
- To liaise with, consult with, and provide information to parents and the wider community on matters relating to the curriculum as required.

NB. It's a good idea to attach a list of all the school's policies relating to the curriculum, stating for each one a lead person or group (ie. the appropriate coordinator or staff team), the date originally approved by the governing body, the next review date (annual, bi-annual, etc. – you don't have to review every policy every year) and who should be consulted before changes are agreed (ie. which members of staff, parents, the school nurse, etc.).

7 Look at displays around school and find out how they link to the curriculum at what stage or level and see how classrooms are set out in different year groups to support learning (you could suggest that governing body and committee meetings are held in different classrooms – size of chairs permitting!)

8 Join in with lessons when invited (but remember that you are not an inspector – follow any existing staff or governor code of practice or protocol that has been adopted).

9 Ask if you can see samples of children's work in different year groups to see what they are actually learning about and achieving (but don't forget confidentiality about individual children) – what does a Level 4 look like?

10 Invite teachers and curriculum coordinators to come to committee or full governing body meetings to talk about their subject when it's relevant to the agenda.

11 Attend special events (assemblies, sports days, concerts, awards ceremonies, etc.), accompany school trips and visit school when something unusual is happening such as a visit from a touring drama group.

12 Participate in governor training/development relating to the curriculum and/or ask if you may attend staff development sessions concerning your area of interest (eg. literacy strategy update if you are the Literacy Governor).

13 Invite members of staff to join the governors for a drink before a full governing body meeting for a chat or organise a joint work/social event around a particular theme.

14 Talk to the children about what they like doing and what they are learning about – try sitting down to eat a school dinner or your sandwiches with them.

15 Most importantly – show an interest, offer your support, talk to adults and children about 'our' school and enjoy joining in with events that celebrate the school's success.

Hints & Tips

Ask if 'the wonderful work done with the children by the visiting sculptress' is on display so everyone can celebrate the children's achievements.

Provision for 3- to 5-year-olds

Although children do not by law have to attend school until the beginning of the term after their fifth birthday, most schools provide education for children before they are five. Every 4-year-old in the country is now entitled to free part-time education and there are also free places for some 3-year-olds depending on their parents' circumstances. Parents can send their children to a local primary school that provides for under-5s, to a state nursery school or children's centre, or they can apply for a nursery grant towards a place at a private playgroup or nursery or with an accredited childminder.

The Foundation Stage

Since September 2000 education provision in all settings for 3- to 5-year-olds has been called the Foundation Stage. Your primary school is likely to provide for the Foundation Stage through a Reception class, or classes, for children aged between 4 and 5 and may also have a Nursery for children from 3 to 4 years old. Even though the Foundation Stage is not compulsory, you are as responsible for ensuring that the money allocated to the school for the 3- and 4-year-olds is used to provide high quality experiences and opportunities for them as you are for children who are 5 or older.

Hints & Tips

Don't forget value for money – 'The new Nursery play area looks great, but how will we know if access to all this expensive equipment really improves the children's physical development?

The Foundation Stage is a distinct stage of learning in its own right but it's also important in preparing children for learning in Key Stage 1. Children learn and develop rapidly in the early years so they need lots of support and stimulation. The government issued *Curriculum Guidance for the Foundation Stage* in May 2000 (DfEE/QCA, 2000), which helps all adults who work with children under 5 (these adults are referred to in the document as 'practitioners' as they are not necessarily qualified teachers) to plan for and meet the diverse needs of all children throughout this stage.

The guidance sets out the aims for the Foundation Stage that underpin all future learning by promoting, supporting and developing children. Principles for early years education are also explained in the document as follows.

- Effective education requires both a relevant curriculum and practitioners who understand and are able to implement the curriculum requirements.
- Early years experience should build on what children already know and can do.
- No child should be excluded or disadvantaged.
- To be effective, an early years curriculum needs to be carefully structured.
- A well-planned and well-organised environment gives children rich and stimulating experiences.
- Practitioners must be able to observe and respond appropriately.
- Children should receive well-planned, purposeful activity and appropriate intervention.
- Practitioners need to ensure that all children feel included, secure and valued.
- Children, parents and practitioners must work together.
- Above all, high-quality care and education by practitioners will lead to effective learning and development for young children.

(Based on DfEE/QCA, 2000, p11)

Documentation about the Foundation Stage stresses the importance of teaching and learning through playing, fun and talking with children as well as forming a partnership with parents.

The Foundation Stage curriculum is organised into six main areas of learning, which are

1. personal, social and emotional development
2. communication, language and literacy
3. mathematical development
4. knowledge and understanding of the world
5. physical development
6. creative development.

Each of these areas has 'early learning goals' that establish expectations for most children to reach by the time they transfer into Year I, which is the beginning of Key Stage 1 of the National Curriculum. Examples are given in the guidance document using 'stepping stones' to show how children learn and make progress towards and beyond the early learning goals.

As a result of the Education Act 2002, the Foundation Stage will become an integral part of the National Curriculum rather than a preparation for it.

Hints & Tips

The way or from whom we learn does not necessarily matter – 'Could we pay one of the teaching assistants extra to show the teachers how to use the new software if the ICT coordinator hasn't got time?'

Assessment

Children do not have to take tests in the Foundation Stage but schools must complete a statutory Foundation Stage Profile, which is a national assessment of every 5-year-old at the end of the stage before they start statutory schooling. For most children, this is at the end of the Reception year in primary school – but profiles are completed in any government-funded setting in which children complete the Foundation Stage. The profile covers all six areas of learning listed above and is based on practitioners' ongoing observations and records. It is done to sum up each child's progress and to plan for and address the child's learning needs. It also provides a basis for recording the progress the child has made between entering Year 1 and when the next statutory assessments are made at the end of Key Stage 1 in Year 2. Children won't know that they are being assessed as no specific assessment activities, tasks or tests are carried out. Practitioners can use completed profiles as their annual report to parents. The profile also provides a consistent approach to assessment of 5-year-olds and allows schools to compare their results to the local and national picture.

Schools that have a Nursery will carry out some form of non-statutory assessment as children enter the class in order to plan their teaching and then they will complete the Foundation Stage Profile before the children transfer from Reception to Year 1.

Inspection

Provision for the under-5s in maintained primary schools is inspected by Ofsted at the same time as the school's statutory provision (now once every six years except in schools causing concern). The inspectors must report on the quality and standards of the education provided in the Foundation Stage, how efficiently the resources are being managed and how well the spiritual, moral, social and cultural development of children is being promoted. They will look for improvement since the previous inspection and, although the guidance mentioned above is not statutory, inspectors will comment on whether or not children are making progress towards the expected goals by the end of the Foundation Stage. If they aren't, the inspectors will identify key issues for improvement in the future.

The National Curriculum

Overview

The purpose of a *national* curriculum is to make sure that all children between the ages of 5 and 16 receive their entitlement to the same range of opportunities for learning, suitable for their age and ability, whatever maintained school they attend anywhere in England. Every school has to record each child's progress and achievements in the same way at the end of each stage of learning and those records must be transferred to the new school when a child moves on. For a summary of how the school curriculum, including the National Curriculum, is organised, see 'How the curriculum is organised' earlier in this chapter.

The National Curriculum for England is set out in detail in two handbooks – one for primary schools (DfEE/QCA, 1999a) and one for secondary (DfEE/QCA, 1999b). The handbooks outline a framework of what must be taught and set attainment targets for learning. In the handbook for primary schools you will find an explanation of the aims, values and purposes (DfEE/QCA, 1999a, p10) underpinning the National Curriculum, along with details of the structure and how it should be developed in schools. In the section on general teaching requirements there is a statement on 'inclusion' that sets out how learning opportunities for all children should be provided with regard to

- setting suitable learning challenges
- responding to children's diverse learning needs
- overcoming potential barriers to learning and assessment for individuals and groups of children.

(DfEE/QCA, 1999a, p30)

The areas of learning in the National Curriculum are divided into core and foundation subjects, which are delivered in four key stages to children from age 5 to 16. Key Stage 1 (Years 1 and 2, from age 5 to 7) and Key Stage 2 (Years 3, 4, 5 and 6, from age 7 to 11) apply to primary schools or in some cases in separate Infant (Years 1 and 2) and Junior (Years 3–6) schools. Key Stages 3 and 4 apply to secondary schools (Years 7 to 11, from age 11 to 16).

The National Curriculum sets out a programme of study for each subject for each key stage. These programmes set out what knowledge, skills and understanding children must be taught. Teachers then choose from a variety of non-statutory schemes of work and guidance to plan how to deliver what must be covered. Children's progress in each subject by the end of Key Stages 1, 2 and 3 is assessed by reference to attainment targets (what children are expected to know, understand and be able to do by the end of each key stage). The attainment targets are expressed as levels of increasing difficulty from 1 to 8 spanning the three key stages. These level descriptors describe the types and ranges of performance that children working at that level should normally demonstrate. The great majority of Key Stages 1 and 2 children are working within Levels 1 to 5. Most children are expected to attain Level 2 by the end of Key Stage 1 and Level 4 by the end of Key Stage 2.

Hints & Tips

Ensure that training comes with new technology – 'The interactive whiteboard looks like a wonderful piece of equipment, but how are members of staff being trained in using it to develop children's skills in different areas of the curriculum?'

This all sounds a bit complicated but you do need to know the basic principles of how the curriculum works to make sense of information and discussions in meetings about how children are progressing through the levels and key stages and how the school is ensuring that standards are being maintained and improved.

Hints & Tips

Think about the quality, not just the quantity, of resources – 'I know every infant classroom would benefit from more story books but would it be a better idea to buy a better range of books and videos and set up an infant library to provide a shared resource?'

Learning across the curriculum

Some themes run through learning across the whole school curriculum, such as developing all children's use of language and information technology and promoting their spiritual, moral, cultural, social, mental and physical development.

Although the National Curriculum is split into core and foundation subjects, teachers in primary schools don't usually teach each subject in isolation as younger children have to develop and refine lots of basic skills in order to learn and make progress. So the structure of the curriculum promotes the teaching of key skills across the whole school curriculum and these are defined in six areas, covering communication, application of number, information technology, working with others, improving own learning and performance and problem-solving (DfEE/QCA, 1999a, p20). The key skills are complemented by thinking skills including information-processing, reasoning, enquiry, creative thinking and evaluation. Teachers have to show in their planning how these skills will be developed.

Example of topic use for cross-curricular learning in Key Stage 2

Key skills
- Communication
- Application of number
- Information technology
- Working with others
- Improving own learning and performance
- Problem-solving

Programme of study for history
- Chronological understanding
- Events, people & changes in the past
- Historical interpretation
- Historical enquiry
- Organisation & communication

ANCIENT EGYPT

History
Time & place
Everyday life
Invasion & warfare
Key people and events
Discoveries, inventions & ideas
Change & influences
Beliefs
Comparative study (ancient/modern)

Geography
Maps
Landscape
Egypt's borders
River Nile
Farming
Environment
Climate
Transport

Science
Water technology
Inventions
Health & medicine
Food & drink
Mummification
Animals
Construction

Music
Evidence of dance
Musical instruments

PSHE & citizenship
Civilisation & society
Working & trading
Values & customs
Kings & Queens
Running the country

Mathematics
Shape, space & measure - pyramids
Data handling - population
Symbols - hieroglyphics

Religious education
Ancient religion
Gods & goddesses
Temples & worships
Priests & priestesses
Mummies, burials & tombs
The afterlife
Bible stories about Egypt
Spiritual & cultural developments

English – language/literature
Reading history text - fiction/non-fiction
Writing and presenting
Commenting and reporting
Researching and using information
Language and hieroglyphics
Speaking, listening and debating
Drama activities

ICT
Use of the internet & software
Searching & researching
Interpreting information
Writing & designing
Investigating
Using graphics & ICT tools

Art & design
Art & artefacts
Architecture
Tomb paintings
Statues
Hieroglyphics
Clothes/textiles

Museum visit to see Egyptian exhibits

Design & technology
Temples
Pyramids
Pottery
Tools & materials
Jewellery

Thinking skills
- Information-processing
- Reasoning
- Enquiry
- Creative thinking
- Evaluation

See the National Curriculum Online: www.nc.uk.net
Choose History, then key phrase/searching, tick Ancient Egypt, choose Key Stage 2, then useful websites and resources to find links to a wealth of useful information and ideas.

A lot of teaching and learning in your school might be done through cross-curricular work. This means that work in different subjects is often closely linked in the form of 'topic'. For instance, when children in Key Stage 2 study a topic about Ancient Egypt, they might not just be doing history. They might also learn about a whole range of other subjects. They might, for instance, be learning about the geography of Egypt and be developing skills in art, design and technology and ICT through painting, making models and using computers. The diagram on the previous page shows examples of some cross-curricular work a teacher might plan around 'Ancient Egypt'.

Hints & Tips

The headteacher's report to governors about curriculum development should be forward looking, not just a list of what has already been done.

The core subjects

The core subjects are English, maths and science. They are compulsory in all four key stages. Teachers must assess children at the end of each key stage in these subjects in order to plot their progress, record their achievements and set targets for the future. Schools do assess children and set targets for other subjects and at other stages but it is not statutory to do so.

English

English is, of course, the most important subject for all children to learn so that they can access all the other subjects of the curriculum, communicate effectively and learn about life. Have a look at the programme of study for English in the National Curriculum handbook to see how the four areas of speaking and listening, reading and writing are covered in Key Stages 1 and 2. QCA suggests that primary schools spend between 24 and 36 per cent of lesson time on English in Key Stage 1 and between 21 and 32 per cent in Key Stage 2 (QCA, 2002 pp35–36).

Most primary schools now use or have adapted the National Literacy Strategy (DfEE, 1998a) to help them plan and teach English. The strategy is not compulsory but is strongly recommended by the government as it was developed from best practice used across the country and is considered to be an effective method of raising standards of achievement. When the strategy was launched in 1998 a programme of training for staff and governors was set up and a whole range of supporting documents were published. See A Literacy Guide for School Governors published by the National Literacy Trust (1998) for more information. Governing bodies were encouraged to appoint a named governor for literacy so your school probably has a 'Literacy Governor'.

Mathematics

Maths in primary school is not just about adding up. In the programmes of study you will see that children learn about using and applying number, shape, space and measures, and (in Key Stage 2) handling data. Skills learned in maths are vital for supporting children's progress in many other subjects, particularly science. To reflect the subject's importance in the curriculum, QCA suggests that between 18 and 25 per cent of lesson time be allocated to maths (QCA, 2002 pp35–36).

Most primary schools are now using or adapting a recommended framework to plan and implement maths called the National Numeracy Strategy (DfEE, 1999a). The strategy focuses on a daily lesson of up to an hour for all children consisting of a high proportion of whole-class teaching with oral and mental work featuring in each lesson. There is a booklet within the Numeracy Strategy package of support documents that you may find helpful called *Information for Governors* (DfEE, 1999b).

Science

Learning about science helps children understand the world around them and how things work. The programme of study covers scientific enquiry, life processes and living things, materials and their properties and physical processes. The science curriculum includes human growth and reproduction and health issues such as the effect of drugs on the body. Parents are not allowed to withdraw their children from these statutory areas of study, as they are from specific sex education lessons. QCA suggests spending 7 per cent of lesson time on science at Key Stage 1 and 9 per cent at Key Stage 2 (QCA, 2002 pp35–36).

Hints & Tips

Beware of raw statistics as you need to know what they mean in the context of your children's progress – 'I know that 80 per cent is in line the national expectation, but that group of children achieved well above the national level in Year 2, so have they made less than the expected progress?'

The foundation subjects

There are seven foundation subjects that must be taught throughout Key Stages 1 and 2. They are history, geography, design and technology, information and communication technology (ICT), art and design, music and physical education (PE). QCA suggests that each of the subjects take up 4 per cent of lesson time at Key Stages 1 and 2, except physical education (for which it suggests 6 per cent at Key Stage 1 and 5 per cent at Key Stage 2) and religious education (for which it suggests 5 per cent of teaching time at Key Stages 1 and 2) (QCA, 2002 pp35–36).

Schools have a lot of flexibility in designing and timetabling their curriculum. They don't have to teach every foundation subject every day or even every week and may choose to deliver some aspects in blocks – such as swimming for Year 2 in the summer term or holding an annual Music Week across Key Stage 2 in the afternoons. However, it is recommended in the government White Paper, *Schools: Achieving Success* (DfES, 2001c) that children do two hours of physical activity every week to support active, healthy lifestyles.

Hints & Tips

Think of practical ways to ensure children with disabilities can access curriculum facilities – 'I know it would mean some disruption but couldn't we move the meeting room upstairs and the library downstairs so the children with mobility difficulties can gain easier access to the library?'

Primary schools don't have to teach modern foreign languages. However, there are non-statutory guidelines in the handbook for use with Year 5 and 6 children for those schools that decide to give children a chance to learn about a language other than English and prepare them for secondary school.

ICT is developing so fast that it's difficult for schools to keep up with the changes and the costs. The National Curriculum requires that schools use ICT to support children's learning in all curriculum areas except PE. As a governor you need to be aware of how your school is developing all children's skills in this area and get involved in supporting effective policy-making, auditing, planning and development of ICT, particularly when it comes to making informed decisions about expenditure. For more about what you should consider and how you can support your school, see the 'ICT checklist' on the next page.

The role of named governors

Governing bodies are encouraged by the DfES to have named governors, particularly for literacy, numeracy, special educational needs, health and safety and looked-after children (children in public care). It's a good idea to share out the workload as much as possible, so you may choose to have named governors for other areas such as science, as it's a core subject, and ICT, as it has to be used across all subjects and is changing so rapidly. Whichever named governors you have, a few general principles and tasks could apply to their roles. If you are a named governor for a particular aspect of the curriculum, you could

- provide a link between the governing body, its committees as appropriate and relevant members of staff
- get involved in drawing up, monitoring, reviewing and evaluating the school's plans and policies in your area of interest
- meet regularly (possibly termly) with the school coordinator for the subject to discuss current issues and progress
- have an input to discussions about setting targets and identifying areas for improvement
- attend governor/staff training, briefings and meetings to keep up to date with developments in your area
- find out what training and development opportunities and funding are available for members of staff, how they access them and what impact training has had on other staff and on children's learning
- find out how the time and expertise of members of support staff is used to support teachers and children in the area
- consider the use of and need for resources to support children in your subject
- report back and make recommendations to the governing body as appropriate on issues relating to the impact of decisions and spending made in your area and on standards and improvements achieved
- promote liaison with other schools and agencies to support developments in your area
- support the production of user-friendly information for parents on what the school provides and how parents can support their children.

ICT checklist

Except for staff salaries, ICT equipment is probably the most expensive resource you have to provide to support learning across the curriculum. It's up to the governing body to make sure that the school is getting value for money when it makes decisions about expenditure.

Beware of false economies

- ❑ Don't opt for the system offered by the LEA just because it's the cheapest.
- ❑ Cheap, low-speed Internet connections result in classes spending huge amounts of time waiting for web pages to load.
- ❑ If hard disks are too small they won't hold the volume of files generated in a year's use.
- ❑ If you overload inadequate systems they fail and crash.
- ❑ Low-cost systems take time to install and to upgrade individual programs on every computer.
- ❑ Amateur installations and maintenance can mean frustration as children and staff wait for lost files to be found and repairs to be done.
- ❑ Your ICT coordinator and teachers are not technicians – pay teachers to teach and technicians to provide technical support.

Before buying ICT equipment

- ❑ Audit current provision, analyse need and draw up a projected expenditure plan that includes the provision of infrastructure, hardware, software, technical support and training.
- ❑ Consider the need for ICT facilities to support management and administration as well as providing equipment for children to access the curriculum.
- ❑ Check the Ofsted report on your LEA's ICT provision.
- ❑ Take professional advice and look at various options before making costly decisions.
- ❑ Invite competitive tenders against high-quality specifications.
- ❑ Buy quality packages that include a wide range of facilities such as capability to run high-speed Internet applications, enough hard disk space to run mainstream software, CD-writers, good graphics, sound facilities, etc.
- ❑ Look into what hardware other schools have been using and discuss the advantages and disadvantages of different systems.
- ❑ Choose a technical support package that covers all situations and guarantees a quick response time.
- ❑ Look into getting together with other schools to share adequate professional technical support.
- ❑ Make sure training is relevant and supports all appropriate members of staff.

Using the Internet and email

The Internet and use of email have enormous potential for enhancing teaching and learning but schools must be aware of the problems and dangers that access to such a wide range of information and communication facilities present for both children and adults. Your governing body should agree an Internet access statement or policy that spells out what all adults and children who access the Internet may and may not do. The policy should be signed by all users and cover issues such as the following.

- ❑ Confidentiality – use of passwords, protecting user identities, parental consent.
- ❑ Legal – copyright, data protection, libel and downloading of illegal material.
- ❑ Ethical – promotion of responsible and appropriate use to children and adults.
- ❑ Technical – introducing viruses to equipment via email and floppy disks.
- ❑ Management – using the Internet for personal reasons, monitoring Internet usage.

Further information and guidance

British Educational Communications and Technology Agency (BECTa) – www.becta.org.uk

British Computer Society (BCS) – www.bcs.org.uk

National Grid for Learning (NGFL) – www.ngfl.org.uk

The Parents' Information Network (PIN) – www.pin.org.uk

Childnet International – www.childnet-int.org

Other statutory and recommended provision

Religious education and collective worship

All maintained schools must provide religious education (RE) and collective worship for all children. RE is not determined by a national curriculum but on a local basis. Your LEA has a Standing Advisory Council on Religious Education (SACRE) made up of people who represent teachers, local churches and faiths groups in the area. The SACRE decides on an agreed syllabus for all schools to follow in its area, although this doesn't apply to voluntary aided schools and those with a religious character – they make their own arrangements. The syllabus must reflect mainly Christian traditions but take account of the teaching and practices of the other principal religions represented in the country. If you are a governor of a voluntary aided, voluntary controlled or foundation school, see the appropriate DfES *Guide to the Law for School Governors* to find out how the rules apply differently.

Acts of collective worship must be broadly Christian in nature and take place daily. This doesn't mean that your school has to have a full assembly every day, as the act of worship may take place in a class or small group and can be led by any adult. Your school should have a policy that sets out when and how children worship and how the school ensures that it's appropriate to the family background, age and ability of the children. Find out how your school uses collective worship to develop shared values and considers spiritual and moral issues with the children. Children should be encouraged to reflect on their own beliefs and respond to the worship offered.

If most or all of the children in your school are not Christian, the headteacher, after consulting with parents and the governing body, can apply to your local SACRE to have the Christian content requirement lifted in order that worship may be distinctively of a particular faith other than Christianity.

Parents can ask for their children to be partly or wholly excused from RE lessons and acts of worship, without necessarily giving a reason, and the school must comply. Parents also have the right to request permission for their child to attend RE and collective worship at a nearby school of any category where a different syllabus is used that more closely matches the parents' choice. Schools are responsible for supervising any children who are withdrawn unless they are lawfully receiving RE or taking part in worship elsewhere.

It's up to the governing body with the headteacher and the LEA to make sure that the local requirements for RE and collective worship are met in full and made accessible to all children, and that parental choice is addressed wherever reasonable.

PSHE and citizenship

Although provision of PSHE and citizenship is not compulsory in primary schools, the National Curriculum handbook provides a framework and guidelines for delivering provision to children in Key Stages 1 and 2. The introduction to this area in the handbook states that

> PSHE and citizenship help to give pupils the knowledge, skills and understanding they need to lead confident, healthy, independent lives and to become informed, active and responsible citizens. Pupils are encouraged to take part in a wide range of activities and experiences across and beyond the curriculum, contributing fully to the life of their school and communities. In doing so they learn to recognise their own worth, work well with others and become increasingly responsible for their own learning.
> (DfEE/QCA, 1999a p136)

All schools support children's development in these areas to a greater or lesser degree through many of the learning opportunities and experiences offered during and beyond the school day. Schools rarely have dedicated lessons in, for instance, citizenship or social education, because such learning is general and cross-curricular. For example, the guidelines advise schools to teach Key Stage 2 children to

- take responsibility for looking after the school environment
- feel positive about themselves by producing a portfolio of achievements
- participate in the school's decision-making process
- make real choices and decisions about issues affecting their health and well-being
- meet and talk with people who contribute to society, such as police officers
- develop relationships through work and play by taking part in activities with groups that have particular needs
- consider social and moral dilemmas that they come across in life, such as encouraging respect between races and dealing with harassment
- prepare for change such as transferring to secondary school.

(DfEE/QCA, 1999a p141)

Find out how your school integrates learning in these and many other aspects through various subjects, activities and special initiatives. For instance, many schools are involved in the National Healthy School Standard, which is an initiative that supports targets for improving the health and well-being of both children and adults in school. The initiative focuses on areas such as drug education, emotional health, healthy eating, physical activity, safety and relationships. Your LEA has a partnership with the local health authority and other agencies and together they have to run a local Healthy Schools Programme and provide funding to support initiatives.

A valuable way of supporting citizenship and giving children responsibility and independence is through the establishment of a school council. Most secondary schools have had school councils for some time and it's becoming increasingly common for primary schools to set up and run class and whole-school councils. Councils give all children a democratic forum to express their views and become involved in decisions that have a genuine input in their school's development and improvement. Governing bodies can play an important part in supporting councils by nominating a governor to be a link person to provide feedback and information or even to act as an independent facilitator at council meetings. As a governor, if you know what the children in your school think about their environment and opportunities for learning and their likes and dislikes, you'll make better informed decisions about things that have a real impact on their daily lives.

Some schools use circletime to promote emotional literacy, solve problems and mediate in conflict situations. Circletime is often established as a lead-up to setting up a school council and is an excellent way of encouraging children to participate and communicate effectively, develop language and respect each other's views. There are plenty of resources available for schools about how councils and circletime support PSHE and citizenship, including a website – www.schoolcouncils.org.

Sex and relationship education

Governing bodies of maintained primary schools must decide whether sex education should be provided and, if so, what it should consist of and how it should be organised. Find out about the situation in your school, look at the policy, see how it fits in with the general framework for PSHE and ask when it was last discussed by governors. The provision of sex education can be a contentious issue so you should take account of the views of staff, parents, health professionals such as the school nurse, and other interested parties before making your decisions. DfES guidance issued in 2000 on sex and relationship education gives advice on how to develop a policy, what lessons should involve and a range of related issues including partnership with parents. Elements of human growth and reproduction that are taught as part of the science curriculum are compulsory, but parents are allowed to withdraw their children from specific sex education lessons. Parents must be given access to the school's policy and it's good practice to provide parents with an opportunity to view and discuss the books, videos and other materials to be used with children.

Drugs education

It isn't compulsory to have a drugs education policy but it's strongly recommended by the DfES (2001a) so that the school's role in drug prevention and education is clear and appropriate to the children's age and needs. Education about the effect of drugs on the human body is included in the science curriculum, but having a wider-reaching policy ensures that there is a whole-school approach to awareness raising and dealing with incidents of drug misuse and abuse.

Drugs include legal substances such as alcohol, nicotine and prescribed medicines as well as illegal drugs. If your governing body has agreed a drugs education policy, make sure that it links in with other policies such as those for PSHE, behaviour, exclusion and health and safety. You should consult all interested parties when drafting a policy about drugs and take advice from experts, particularly about legal matters. Guidance documents produced by the Standing Conference on Drug Abuse (SCDA) called *The Right Choice*, *The Right Responses* and *The Right Approach* are available free from the DfES.

Curriculum enrichment

Addressing the needs of the whole child

The curriculum isn't just a collection of subjects. Most schools offer a range of opportunities beyond the statutory and recommended activities to encourage children to learn and develop their talents. You have a great deal to contribute when it comes to supporting the wider curriculum and addressing the needs of the whole child.

Visitors to school and off-site visits

Visitors to school and off-site visits are important opportunities to enrich the curriculum. They extend the breadth of opportunities and experiences offered to the children through their contacts with the wider community.

The headteacher usually proposes what off-site visits should take place and whom to invite into school to talk to, and work with, the children and the staff in order to complement and enrich the curriculum. Governors' support, both financial and through their links with the wider community, aims to extend the breadth of opportunities and experiences offered to the children.

No charge can be made for curriculum-related activities during school session times, but parents can be invited to make contributions as long as it is made clear that the children of parents who don't contribute will not be treated differently. Music tuition is an exception to the rule, as charges may be made for an individual child or groups of up to four children. The governing body must agree a charging policy to explain what charges will be made for activities out of session times and an off-site visits policy is recommended (see DfEE, 1998b). Your LEA will provide guidance on charges and regulations relating to trips and residential visits. When discussing provision relating to visitors and off-site trips you should consider issues such as the following.

- How much is the visitor/visit going to cost and can the school afford it with/without voluntary contributions?
- How does the visitor/visit support the curriculum and provide added value to the children's learning? (For example, a trip to a French theme park could be hard to justify in comparison with several local museum visits.)
- Have visitors and those supervising off-site visits been police-checked? (All employees and unpaid volunteers including governors having contact with children are subject to a criminal record check by the Criminal Records Bureau (CRB). LEAs act as the registered body for maintained schools and should have informed schools of procedures. For detailed information about the CRB disclosure service, see www.disclosure.gov.uk.)
- Is the ratio of adults to children appropriate for off-site supervision?
- What transport is to be used and are safety precautions adequate (eg. seat belts on buses)?
- What information is given to parents about trips and is their permission sought for children to be taken off-site?
- Have arrangements for emergency contacts and procedures been made and is all necessary insurance in place?
- Is the trip accessible to all children in the relevant year group? (For example, has wheelchair access been arranged?)

Depending on your LEA's particular policies and guidance, you probably delegate to the headteacher the responsibility for approving visits and visitors, although you will almost certainly

Hints & Tips

Check the health and safety implications of curriculum decisions – 'It would be great to take up the offer of free use of the high school's science laboratories, but how would we ensure the safety of 30 children if only one adult is available to supervise them?'

need to sanction the arrangements for any residential journey.

For more about charging for school activities, see Chapter 7, 'Finance'.

Out-of-school-hours provision

Clubs and activities at lunchtime, before and after school hours, and in holidays are offered in many schools but attendance must be voluntary as staff can't be compelled to provide such activities. The governing body controls the use of the school premises outside hours in line with LEA guidance. Governors may decide to pay members of staff extra to provide additional activities such as netball sessions or an after-school homework club, or they may allow other agencies to provide opportunities for children and/or adults on the premises at weekends or in the holidays. Also, if your school is part of an Education Action Zone or Excellence in Cities programme, you should take advantage of any support and resources on offer for curriculum enrichment and extra-curricular activities.

Providing a quality learning environment

The school curriculum is enriched when children and adults work in an attractive and stimulating learning environment. You should consider the impact of your decisions on the school environment and make sure that expenditure on such items as extending the premises or developing the school grounds positively promotes learning. For instance, don't just resurface the playground – discuss developing an outdoor classroom with seating, landscaping and a wild-flower area and involve the children in the planning. Make sure that resources in classrooms and communal areas are adequate to meet the needs of the curriculum. Storage facilities should provide easy access to resources for children and staff while having regard to health and safety issues. Displays of children's work in classrooms, corridors, entrance halls and so on should reflect the curriculum and celebrate the achievements and talents of all the children.

Partnership with parents

By law, governing bodies must provide certain information to parents about the curriculum and their children's achievements. But real partnership is about involving parents in supporting their children's education. Wherever possible, governors should consult parents before making decisions that will have an impact on their children's learning and welfare. Parents should be made aware of their rights and have opportunities to discuss their children's needs and progress with staff. You can promote partnership by making sure that the important role of parents is emphasised in school policies and that decisions about matters such as homework take account of the views of parents.

For more about partnership with parents, see the 'Parents' chapter.

The role of support staff

Members of the support staff make a vital contribution to curriculum delivery and learning. The governing body is responsible for deciding how many staff to employ and at what level. Therefore, you should find out about the roles that teaching assistants, learning support staff, special needs workers, learning mentors, nursery nurses, lunchtime supervisors and others play in your school. You need to know how these employees work alongside teachers to address the needs of individual children and raise standards overall. Not only does this help you to understand what happens in school and how children's learning is encouraged, it also helps you to make decisions about staffing levels.

Developing links with other schools, agencies and organisations

Staff from local services such as education welfare, educational psychology, special needs and school nursing provide valuable support to schools, particularly in helping to reduce barriers to learning so children can access the curriculum. You may have to support the headteacher in securing additional provision or funding so that children can benefit from such services.

Primary schools don't operate in isolation and can enhance the curriculum and improve standards of teaching and learning by working with other local

schools, and especially those with beacon and specialist status. Staff can share expertise and resources and organise joint events to enable children to meet and work together. You can help to develop links with other schools and also with a range of other organisations and agencies that contribute towards children's learning. You should consider the need to buy in additional services as necessary to advise staff, provide training and enhance the curriculum.

Transition issues

Children can find it difficult to settle into a new school or to transfer from one stage of education to the next. They need continuity in their learning and consistent support for their pastoral needs in order to benefit from all the available experiences and opportunities. Schools must, by law, transfer certain information about children's needs and their achievements when they move from one school to another but it's also important to make transition from one year group or key stage to the next as smooth as possible. You can find out how your school addresses the curriculum and other needs of children at transition by asking the following questions.

- What arrangements are made to find out as much as possible about each child's abilities and needs when they first arrive in school? (For example, by talking to parents, analysing information from a previous school or pre-school setting, assessing reports about special needs from health professionals.)
- What advice is given to parents to help them settle their children into school? (In a Nursery or year group booklet, for example, that sets out the routines and expectations specific to that year of education.)
- What support is available for children who arrive in school with little or no understanding of English? (Availability of interpreters and translated materials for parents.)
- What information is transferred about each child from one year to the next to inform their new teacher of their abilities and needs? (What time and opportunities are there for teachers to discuss individual children as well as sharing statutory records?)
- How are children prepared for the changes they will face at secondary school and what information is given to parents? (Do children visit the 'link' secondary schools, and do staff from the link schools come into your school to work with Year 6?)

For more about transferring school records, see Chapter 4, 'Children'.

From planning to raising achievement

Planning curriculum delivery

The National Curriculum document tells schools broadly what children should be taught in each subject but the finer detail and how it should be delivered is up to the individual school. Each governing body has to agree broadly what is to be included in the whole school curriculum and decide how a balanced curriculum is going to be provided, taking account of the social and economic context of the school and the circumstances and needs of the children. This is done through the curriculum and other policies such as those for teaching and learning, homework and marking.

Using a wealth of guidance and information available from government departments, the LEA, commercial organisations and colleagues, the teachers have to plan the detailed curriculum based on the principles laid down by the governors. Long-, medium- and short-term plans covering subject and cross-curricular themes are drawn up, probably using a common school format. Plans for individual children who have special needs and/or behavioural difficulties also have to be drawn up and incorporated into the daily lessons. It's important that activities are planned so that each child is working at their correct level. Supply teachers and those standing in for colleagues need to be able to deliver a lesson at short notice by picking up the appropriate plan.

To better understand how this complex planning works in your school, ask to see examples of plans and if possible join in with a lesson. Then you can track from the long-term plan to the daily one to see the outcome of the planning process.

Assessment, recording and reporting

Assessment is an integral part of teaching and learning and provides information to teachers, parents and children about how a child is progressing. Assessment isn't just about formally measuring what children know or are able to do at a certain point in their education, it's also used day to day to improve teaching and learning and raise children's standards of achievement.
This is often referred to as formative assessment. The objectives are to

- share learning goals with children and help them recognise the standard to aim for
- provide feedback for children to identify what they should do to improve
- involve both teachers and children in reviewing and reflecting on performance and progress.

Attainment targets and level descriptions

At the back of the National Curriculum document is a section called 'Attainment targets'. These, as described in the Education Act 1996, set out the knowledge, skills and understanding that children of different abilities and maturities are expected to have by the end of each key stage. Attainment targets consist of a series of level descriptors of increasing difficulty. Each level descriptor describes the types and range of performance children working at that level should characteristically demonstrate.

The National Curriculum levels have been designed so that most children will progress approximately one level every two years. The level expected for most children at the end of Key Stage 1 is a Level 2, which is split into Level 2C, Level 2B and Level 2A (where A is the highest). By the end of Key Stage 2, most children are expected to reach Level 4.

In deciding on a child's level of attainment teachers have to assess which description best fits the child's performance. The purpose of this assessment is to help to improve standards through giving teachers information about the needs and abilities of their children. This information will help them in planning work, and in identifying areas in which some children face particular challenges.

It's possible for children in your school to obtain a range of levels in each end of key stage assessment. At Key Stage 1 the top level a child can achieve is Level 4 and at Key Stage 2 the top level that can be achieved is a Level 6.

All teachers should keep detailed records of assessments, of their work with the class and of individual children's activities and progress. The teachers use these records to draw up the reports that must be written at least once each year on every child and sent to their parents for information and discussion.

Governors have to make sure that statutory teacher assessment is carried out for every child at the end of each stage. A Foundation Stage Profile is completed when children are 5 years old – see the section on 'Provision for 3- to 5-year-olds' earlier in this chapter. At the end of Key Stage 1 in Year 2 and Key Stage 2 in Year 6, children have to be assessed in English, maths and science. However, teachers also assess children at regular intervals in all areas of learning, not just the core subjects. You need to decide how much information you want the headteacher to provide about assessment results for you to be able to monitor standards and progress.

Testing

As well as teacher assessment, governors must make sure that the school is meeting the statutory requirements for testing children at the end of each key stage. At the end of Key Stage 1 children have to do National Curriculum tasks and tests in English and mathematics and they take tests in English, mathematics and science at the end of Key Stage 2. These tests are popularly (but not officially) known as SATs.

Children's results of teacher assessments and tests and tasks must be reported to their parents and you must make sure that the overall percentages of achievements in Key Stages 1 and 2 are sent to the LEA. Every year you must also publish results in the school prospectus and the governing body's annual report to parents (except if 10 or fewer children took the tests). The overall Key Stage 2 results for every school in England are published nationally and are often referred to as league tables. However, the Key Stage 1 results, although collated by the DfES, are not published nationally.

The assessments and tests help teachers to find out about children's strengths and weaknesses and determine what they know about a subject and at what level they are working. It is expected that most children will achieve attainment Level 2 in the core subjects by the end of Key Stage 1 and Level 4 by the end of Key Stage 2. Many schools use optional National Curriculum tests at the end of Years 3, 4 and 5 in order to complement regular assessments and gather evidence of children's progress. You will find it useful to know what tests are used and to discuss an analysis of the results to help you understand how targets are set.

See the chapter 'School improvement' for details about your responsibilities in reporting test results.

References

Advisory Centre for Education (ACE) and the National Early Years Network (2000) *Education and the Under-Eights: A Guide to the Law* (4th edition). London: National Early Years Network.

DfEE (1998a) *The National Literacy Strategy: Framework for Teaching.* London: DfEE.

DfEE (1998b) *Health and Safety on Educational Visits: Good Practice Guide.* London: DfEE.

DfEE (1999a) *The National Numeracy Strategy: Framework for Teaching Mathematics from Reception to Year 6*. London: DfEE.

DfEE (1999b) *The National Numeracy Strategy: Information for Governors*. London: DfEE.

DfEE/QCA (1999a) *The National Curriculum – Handbook for Primary Teachers in England*. London: TSO.

DfEE/QCA (1999b) *The National Curriculum – Handbook for Secondary Teachers in England*. London: TSO.

DfEE/QCA (2000) *Curriculum Guidance for the Foundation Stage*. London: DfEE and QCA.

DfES (2000) *Sex and Relationship Education*. London: DfES.

DfES (2001a) *A Guide to the Law for School Governors – Community Schools (Primary)*. London: DfES.

DfES (2001b) *National Training Programme for New Governors*. London: DfES.

DfES (2001c) *Schools: Achieving Success*. London: TSO.

National Literacy Trust (1998) *A Literacy Guide for School Governors.* London: National Literacy Trust.

Ofsted (1999) *Handbook for Inspecting Primary and Nursery Schools*. London: TSO.

QCA (2002) *Designing and Timetabling the Primary Curriculum: A Practical Guide*. London: QCA.

Useful websites

www.dfes.gov.uk
General Department for Education and Skills site. Information for governors, teachers, parents and jobseekers and links to lots of other useful sites.

www.nc.uk.net
National Curriculum Online. All National Curriculum documents and guidance, teaching resources.

www.schoolcouncils.org
National School Council Organisation. Information and support on setting up and running school councils.

www.ofsted.gov.uk
Ofsted. Information and publications.

www.ace-ed.org.uk
Advisory Centre for Education. Information and advice for governors and parents.

www.hmso.gov.uk
Her Majesty's Stationery Office. Information and publications on all legislation.

www.teachernet.gov.uk
DfES site for people working in schools. Teaching and learning, professional development, management, research, resources.

www.tes.co.uk
The *Times Educational Supplement*. News, information, links, on-line resources.

www.learn.co.uk
The Guardian education site. News, information, links, on-line resources.

www.ngc.org.uk
National Governors' Council. Run by governors for governors – advice, information, publications.

www.ncsl.org.uk
National College for School Leadership. Information, support and training for senior managers in schools.

www.nagm.org.uk
National Association of Governors and Managers. Information and training for governors and managers, publications.

www.teachernet.com
Commercial organisation. Curriculum guidance, classroom resources, links, discussion boards.

School improvement

Graham Reeves, Pat Brunton, Jill Bostock, Catherine Baird

Your strategic overview

The governing body is responsible for making sure that children receive a high-quality education that is continuously improving. All aspects of school life contribute to this – the people, the premises, the standards of teaching and learning and the local community. Financial decisions on any of these aspects of school life must contribute to school improvement in its broadest sense. To help you manage this process you will need to think about the vision, mission, values, aims, policies and plans for your school.

Vision, mission and values

Your school vision or mission statement sums up your view of the purpose of the school. In establishing or reviewing the vision, everyone involved with the school needs to think about where you want the school to be in five to ten years' time and about how you are going to get there. Don't forget you are building on the past and moving on from the present.

As governors you will be involved in reviewing the vision and mission of the school from time to time. This is an effective way of reminding everybody of the school's main purposes and its role in the local community. All too easily this big picture can be lost in the day-to-day challenges of helping a school to run effectively.

Thinking about and discussing your vision and mission helps you to define the values that are important to you and which you would wish to see supporting every aspect of the life of the school. The vision or mission statement for your school can be supported by a set of values that define the important things that will always be taken into consideration when reaching a decision on any matter. By spending time agreeing your values, you are laying down the basis of an agreed way of working throughout all aspects of school life. This will be a great help to you in situations where there are difficult decisions to make.

Among the values you will want to consider are

- equality of opportunity
- mutual respect
- openness to change
- quality assurance
- the right to individual development
- value for money
- long-term sustainability.

If it's obvious that these values underpin all the decisions that you make as a governing body, it will help everyone to feel more comfortable that they have made the right decision, and to be more confident to defend the decision if anyone challenges them.

Vision and mission are often used to mean the same thing. Elsewhere – and perhaps more correctly – they have distinct meanings. Strictly, vision deals with the future and mission with the present.

Vision statement

A vision statement would be about what you want to achieve and might describe the situation you will be in when you have achieved it. For example

> Within five years the school will be widely recognised as providing the highest-quality education in a state-of-the-art facility.

Mission statement

A mission statement, on the other hand, would be about what the school does and what it offers on a day-to-day basis. For example

> The mission of the school is to provide all children with opportunities to fulfil their potential academically, socially and physically.

You should try to consult all members of the school community about the school's vision, mission and values and give them an opportunity to contribute their definition. But after that, members of the governing body have a particular role as guardians of this vision. You are responsible for making sure that all aspects of school development support it.

Refer to your vision, mission and values as often as you can. Quote them in policies, school brochures, job descriptions and at every opportunity. Display them around the school. They should become something that everyone recognises and knows and they should become a reference point for everything you do. The world changes, so your statements will need to change. Keep them under review but don't expect to change them more often than every three or four years – and then try to keep changes to a minimum. They give everyone a sense of direction – and you don't want that direction to be always changing.

Hints & Tips

Policies provide for a degree of consistency about the things that really matter – and particularly about children's learning.

Aims

A set of aims fleshes out the vision and mission and describe in broad terms what you want to achieve in any particular development area. Aims represent an indication of intent. They need to be clear, to be understood by all and should underpin all decisions you make. All school policies and plans should show how the aims of your school are to be achieved.

School aims build on the vision and mission. They really say the same thing but in more detail. Perhaps the best way of producing a set of aims is for a small group of people – governors and school staff – to have a brainstorming session and to come up with a first draft that is then given to other people for their comments. You will probably go through a number of drafts and the important thing is to finish with something that most – and preferably all – people can subscribe to.

Together the vision and/or mission statement and the school aims provide the basis for a degree of consistency within the school about the things that matter. Without them it would be difficult for anyone to know for sure what does matter for your school and what is expected of them.

Policies

Policies are descriptions of principles, expectations and procedures. Anyone reading a written policy will know what the line is on any particular issue, and will know what they – or anyone else – is expected to do in particular circumstances. Policies are what gives any organisation its coherence and stops it from being a loose grouping of people with little in common.

Policies might be written by the headteacher, members of the school staff, individual governors, committees or working parties. They should be drawn up following consultation with a wide cross-section of the school community. However they are produced it is the full governing body who has to approve and adopt them.

Policies are there to guide the actions everyone takes to fulfil the aims of the school and act as a point of reference against which you make decisions. They are there to give clarity and consistency about how your school operates, telling everyone what to expect and what is expected of them. You should make your policies known to, and understood by, everybody.

It makes sense to review policies every two or three years to make sure they are still appropriate. Try to spread out the review dates so that you don't have to do everything at the same time. Sometimes, however, you need to change a review date because of circumstances such as a change in the law or a particular decision that has a knock-on effect.

All policies should still be as short and as clear as possible although they might be supported by other materials. Remember that long documents take a long time to produce and very often don't get read. Make sure that your policies deal with the things that really matter.

It's a good idea for you to have a simple standard format for policy documents. They might, for instance, be organised under the headings 'general principles', 'what we do' and 'date for review'. For another policy format, see 'A model policy proforma' on the next page.

There are some policies that you must have as governors. A full list of legally required and

A model policy pro forma

POLICY TITLE: ....

Date adopted by the governing body: ....

Contact person: ....

Rationale:
(Why do we need this policy? What is its legal status? What background information do we have? How does it reflect the vision and values of the school?)

Aims and objectives:
(How do these relate to the school's vision, aims and improvement plan targets?)

Roles and responsibilities:
(Who does what?)

Action to be taken:

Who will be responsible for monitoring? ....

Review date: ....

recommended policies and publications is available in Annexes 3 and 4 of *A Guide to the Law for School Governors* (DfES, 2001).

School development and improvement plans

For quite a number of years, many schools have had school development plans. More recently an increasing number of schools have had school improvement plans. There is a need for both types of plan – although the difference isn't always clear and many schools incorporate the two.

There is so much to be done in a school that it's very easy for people to get totally overwhelmed. Many things can get overlooked and, often, unimportant things can get done while more important ones get missed.

That's why school development plans came into use. They were a way of dealing with the multitude of tasks facing a school. They helped headteachers stay in control and helped everyone identify the priorities. Development plans have had a great effect and have brought a little order out of the potential chaos.

The only trouble was that school development plans didn't necessarily focus on learning – the single most important activity in a school. There were so many tasks, such as reorganising the library, replacing desks, ordering books and producing documents, that learning often got missed out. That's not to say that all the other things don't have an effect on learning, but the effect is often indirect or unclear.

What people began to realise was that schools really need to have a systematic approach to improving children's learning. They needed to plan what they were going to do to have a direct and discernible effect on what and how children learned – enter the school improvement plan.

You need a plan that deals with the ongoing details of school management. You also need one that deals with improving learning. *The school development plan deals with general management, whereas the school improvement plan deals with learning.*

A school development plan helps the headteacher and others manage the school. It helps everyone to keep things working. A school improvement plan helps you, the headteacher and others to lead the school.

The school development plan

The school development plan deals with the management and development of all aspects of school life. It's an essential tool that helps you to understand how all the various developments in the school fit together in a coordinated way to support the overall vision and aims of the school.

The usual areas covered in a school development plan include the curriculum, staffing, premises and community links, but your plan may well have other areas of priority depending on your particular circumstances. Plans usually cover a three-year period and should be costed to make it clear how the spending decisions made in the school support the agreed development priorities. You are likely to plan Year One in some detail. Year Two will be planned in outline, and for Year Three you will probably have a list of priorities for action. This structure recognises how priorities within a school can change either for internal reasons or due to new local and national government initiatives. Each year you will want to review the plan, add more detail to what will now be the new Year One, and look further into the future.

For the areas of development within Year One you need to decide what actually needs to be done, who is responsible for the action, by when, and at what cost. Some of the actions will be your responsibility as governors, others will be carried out by members of the school staff.

Because the school development plan covers the full range of school activities, you will want to consult as many people as possible about its contents. Whoever actually does the final drafting, it will need to be based on information, suggestions and even bids from teachers, support staff, individual governors, governing body committees and perhaps the PTA and the children. You also need to take into consideration any national or local initiatives that are likely to affect your school. The resulting plan has to be approved

School development plan

Area for priority	Intended outcomes	Activities	Personnel	Resources	Costs	Timescale	Monitoring arrangements

by the full governing body. It becomes binding on everyone and provides the basis for establishing the school budget. See Chapter 7, 'Finance'.

As governors you have a particularly important role to play in monitoring the overall progress of the school development plan. Your plan should therefore identify what you intend to measure to monitor progress, who is going to do this and when and how they are going to report back to the governing body.

See the sample format for a school development plan on the previous page.

Hints & Tips

As governors you have a particularly important role to play in monitoring the overall progress of the school development plan.

The school improvement plan

Targets

A school improvement plan has a number – usually a small number – of targets related to the improvement of children's learning. These targets should be as clear and as specific as possible. They might be either instructional or expressive.

Instructional targets explicitly identify their own outcomes. For example, 'To ensure that 85 per cent of children achieve Level 4 or above in science by the end of Year 6' is an instructional target. At the end of Year 6 it will be relatively easy to know whether or not it has been achieved.

In *expressive* targets the outcomes are not so specifically defined. For example, 'To improve children's appreciation of music' is an expressive target. It won't be particularly obvious whether or not it has been achieved. You'll need something else to help you make the judgement. What you have to do is describe how you will know whether the target has been reached. You might, for example, decide that you'll get children to list the music they like, and will be satisfied if half of them mention – somewhere in their list – music from another country. You need such success criteria for expressive targets but not for instructional targets. Just because something is not easily measurable doesn't mean that it can't form a valuable target.

Activities

Your school improvement plan will also identify a number of activities. These are the things that you will do in order to achieve the targets. Be careful – it's very easy to confuse activities with targets. You might have a target concerned with the improvement of children's reading. An activity to help you achieve that target might be to restock the library. Restocking the library isn't itself a target for the school improvement plan, although it might well be in the school development plan. It's a means to an end. The target is about improving children's learning. An activity is one of the ways in which you'll make that improvement happen.

It's a good idea if your school improvement plan identifies who is responsible for doing what, the timescale involved and the resources – and their cost – needed. You will probably also want to say when the target will be reviewed and by whom.

Because of its professional and technical nature you will probably expect the school improvement plan to be drawn up by the headteacher in consultation with the school staff. You should still have an input, however – identifying priorities, making sure that targets are challenging but realistic, and making sure that they are based on evidence.

See the sample format for a school improvement plan on the next page.

Hints & Tips

The target is about improving children's learning. An activity is one of the ways in which you'll make that improvement happen.

The government has outlined a model for setting targets for children's performance, which is referred to as the 'five-stage cycle of school improvement' (DfEE, 1998 p62). The cycle encourages you and your headteacher to review and improve school performance.

Stage I How well are we doing?

You need clear information about your school's performance in terms of what children are achieving. You can get the information from such sources as the headteacher's report and from a comparison of results from National Curriculum assessments with performance in previous years. Because differences in intake lead to some variations, emphasis is now often given to 'value added' measurements. At the end of the Foundation Stage children are assessed so that each child's progress and learning needs can be gauged. This assessment, called the Foundation Stage Profile, summarises what each child knows, understands and can do in relation to the early learning goals. From the information provided it's possible to measure how children of any ability are progressing and thus, from subsequent assessments, to consider the 'value added' aspect of their progress, rather than data that just indicate what levels have been reached.

School improvement plan

Target	Activity	Personnel	Resources	Timescale	Success criteria (if appropriate)	Monitoring arrangements	Notes

Stage 2 How do we compare with similar schools?

You need to consider how well your school is doing in the wider context of the performances achieved by other similar schools. In order to do this, you need information about the performance of similar schools in terms of their children's achievements using a common set of performance criteria such as the proportion of children achieving the expected National Curriculum level or better at the end of Key Stages 1 and 2. This information helps you to think about how better-performing schools achieve their results and whether anything can be learned to raise the standard of achievement of children in your school.

Stage 3 What more can we aim to achieve?

With good information you can set realistic and challenging targets based on analysis of the school's current performance and that of similar schools. Targets are most often set in the autumn term, when you can also review progress towards current targets.

By analysing children's performance as part of an annual cycle of school improvement, you and the school's staff can consider the effectiveness of current teaching practices in the school and identify specific areas of work that could be improved. For instance, a target could be set to improve the percentage of children reaching Level 2 or above in English at the end of Key Stage 1.

The timescales chosen will depend on the nature of the target, the needs of the children and what action is necessary. Targets should be set against timescales that both maintain impetus and, where relevant, are sufficient for new teaching strategies to take effect.

With your strategic overview you may need to consider whether any targets have financial implications such as extra funding to improve resources in a particular area.

Stage 4 What must we do to make it happen?

Once you have set the targets, the school must take determined action to meet them. Targets must then become part of the school improvement plan, linked with these questions.

- What will be done?
- Who will be responsible for ensuring the action takes place?
- What resources, training and support will be needed?
- What will the timetable be?
- When will this be reviewed?

Your main duty as a member of the governing body is to make sure that plans to meet targets are in place and can be resourced.

Stage 5 Making it happen

The school staff have the main responsibility for putting plans into action guided by an action plan. The role of the governing body is to oversee the implementation of the improvement plan, to make sure that regular monitoring takes place and to analyse what is happening and the effect on children's performance. In turn this also helps inform you when you come to set future targets.

Monitoring and evaluation

The governing body is responsible for standards within your school so it's important that you have some level of understanding, not only of the contents of the school development and improvement plans, but also of the school's success with the various targets and activities. Ask your headteacher to include progress with the plans as a regular feature of the termly report. You can also use your visits to the school to focus on specific aspects of development and improvement.

No matter how good and detailed a planning structure you have for your school, and how enthusiastically everyone has been involved in drawing up plans, you won't reap the benefits if you don't know how well you are progressing during the course of the year. Knowing how well you are doing, which targets are being met and which possibly are slipping behind, is crucial information for you to keep track of how things are progressing in your school. You need this information to plan sensibly for the following year. It's the vital evidence that the financial decisions you have made are leading to the improvements you have planned.

If you have been careful about setting priorities and targets, you should have no problem in agreeing what evidence you can collect during the year to show what progress is being made. Agree how you will monitor progress at the time you draw up the plans – it's almost impossible to try to tag on a monitoring system later. Evaluation of this monitoring information, either part-way through or at the end of the year, will give you the baseline for next year's planning.

Setting and publishing National Curriculum targets

Since 1998 governing bodies in primary schools have been responsible for setting and publishing targets for children's performance in the statutory tests at the end of Key Stage 2. You have to set these targets in the autumn term of each year for what children who are currently in Year 5 are expected to achieve when they reach the end of Year 6. In other words, you have to predict what children will be able to do five terms in advance. The targets relate to the percentage of children in the year group who are expected to reach Level 4 or above and Level 5 or above in English and maths tests. In your annual report to parents you must publish targets for the year to which the report relates, for the two previous years and the following year (a four-year comparison), along with corresponding results where they are known.

Your school's targets should be based on an analysis of individual children's previous achievements, current progress and a prediction of what they should be able to do in the future given appropriate support and challenging work. The targets should relate to the average of the actual children in the cohort and their expected progress. For example, a child who gained a Level 2 in their Year 2 assessments would normally be expected to gain a Level 4 in Year 6. If that child is making better than average progress, according to teacher assessments, they might be targeted to gain a Level 5. In this case the school would be seen to have 'added value' if the child reaches the target. You need to be satisfied when targets are presented for approval that they are realistic and not just proposed in order to show an increase of a couple of percentage points on last year's results or to match the national targets. Overall targets could be much higher or even lower than the previous year because the abilities of children in different cohorts can vary widely.

Your targets must be agreed by the LEA, so there might be a certain amount of negotiation. They then contribute to the LEA's overall targets for the primary schools in its area. These are submitted to the DfES and compared with the national targets. The national targets for Key Stage 2 in both English and maths for 2004 are for 85 per cent of children to achieve Level 4 or more and 35 per cent to achieve Level 5 or more. Remember that school that exceeds the national targets is not necessarily raising standards, whereas one whose results are below national average may actually have made enormous improvements over the last few years. There is a great deal of information and data available to tell you how your school is really doing compared with similar schools with children in comparable circumstances.

The target-setting trail

To set targets you need to be aware of the range of information and data available about children's progress and performance nationally, locally and specifically for your school. Although you don't need to look at all the intricate detail, it helps if you know about the sources of information. You might expect the headteacher to propose your targets but it's your responsibility to set them, so you need to be confident that they are both realistic and challenging and that they are based on all the available evidence.

The Autumn Package

Every autumn the DfES produces information on pupil performance in the Autumn Package for each key stage. For Key Stages 1 and 2 the packages contain national results of statutory tests, value-added information and benchmark information. The information helps schools to understand what progress they are making, compare the progress made by individual children with progress made by other children with similar prior attainment and compare their performance with similar schools. Tables and graphs are in many

Four more key points about target-setting

1 Make sure that the school's targets in the core subjects are agreed annually and that they are published in your annual report to parents.

2 Have a strategic overview – considering, for instance, how the target-setting process interlinks with other aspects of your responsibility such as finance and staffing.

3 Link the targets to school improvement planning, supporting the headteacher and staff in working through a cycle of school improvement that concentrates on children's performance.

4 Remember that although the Key Stage 2 results are a measure of performance at the time children leave your school, all children should make good progress during each key stage. Your school will have additional evidence on how individual children perform, which will also help you in the target-setting process.

cases followed by a list of useful questions to help you focus on how your school's results compare with the national data. As each package is about 40 pages long, ask your headteacher initially to show you and talk through the basic information such as the summary tables.

The Performance and Assessment Report (PANDA)

The DfES also sends the headteacher a PANDA report in the autumn term. This contains confidential information specific to your school. You can expect the head to make you aware of the report and use it with the staff to identify areas for improvement and set targets for the future. The report tells you how your results compare to those of schools nationally and to similar schools. It gives a broader overview of the school's context such as the level of special needs and information from the census of population. As the report is over 40 pages long, try starting with discussion of the most useful parts, such as the

- attainment summaries
- graphs that show trends over the last five years in your school
- pages that set out comparisons with national benchmarks for schools in similar contexts based on free school meal entitlement
- tables that show the performance of your boys and girls against national indicators
- glossary of terms.

Each page has an explanation of what the statistics mean and an interpretation of the results.

Other resources

Resources such as analysis tools and a National Summary Data Report (NSDR) are available on the DfES website for schools to use. They allow more detailed comparisons with national information based on inspection evidence in terms of statistics such as pupil–teacher ratios.

LEA information

Your LEA has to provide performance data on all the schools it maintains to complement the national data and to inform schools how they fit into the local picture in terms of achievement. The format of data varies between LEAs, so you might want to ask to see the information that the staff have found most helpful.

School-based information

As well as all the above information, you need to see a copy of any school self-evaluation. Of particular relevance will be analyses of value-added information. For instance, the availability of individual pupil-level data makes it possible for schools to plot the attainment of every child who was in Year 2 against their Year 6 results on a 'Value-added line and progress chart'. This means that you can see how well children who have been in your school throughout Key Stage 2 have actually progressed over the four years, whatever their level of ability. This sort of analysis can tell you if your school is making a real difference to children in comparison with average expectations. It can also highlight issues about the progress made by different groups of children such as those with special needs, those in public care, boys or girls, those who were admitted to the school part-way through the key stage, and children from ethnic minorities or with English as an additional language.

Most importantly, you should ask questions about what the statistics mean in the context of your children, what factors affect children's progress and what the implications are for setting and meeting targets in the future.

References

DfEE (1998) *Supporting the Target Setting Process* London: DfEE.

DfES (2001) *A Guide to the Law for School Governors – Community Schools (Primary)*. London: DfES.

Children

Catherine Baird

It may seem an obvious thing to say, but schools exist for children. More specifically, they exist so that children can learn and develop. Yet it's so easy to get caught up with all the business and busyness of school that you lose sight of what's most important. This chapter focuses on children, their needs and your responsibilities in meeting those needs.

Admissions

Responsibility

Unless yours is a foundation and voluntary aided primary school, the local education authority (LEA) is almost certainly the admission authority. This means that it's responsible for setting the policies and procedures for admitting children to the school. Your role on the governing body is to enter into any consultations and to make sure that the LEA's policies are implemented. Occasionally the LEA can delegate or give over the responsibility to the governing body with your agreement. In foundation and voluntary aided primary schools the governing body is the admission authority.

All those involved in operating admission arrangements must have regard to the School Admissions Code of Practice (DfEE, 1999a) and, where necessary, the School Admission Appeals Code of Practice (DfEE, 1999b), which give guidance on the law and guiding principles for school admissions.

Consultation

Each year the LEA consults you about the arrangements it's proposing for the school. It also consults with other admission authorities such as neighbouring LEAs and governing bodies within what is known as the 'relevant area'. The LEA sets the relevant area for consultation about admission arrangements for each school it maintains and reviews these every two years. Following this consultation the LEA decides on the admission arrangements and notifies each of the admission authorities it has consulted.

Consultation must include all the admission arrangements that the LEA proposes to use for a particular school year.

Admission arrangements should include

- the admissions policy
- the procedures for and timing of applications
- admission numbers and full details of oversubscription criteria and how they will be applied
- any use of interviewing or selection (such arrangements are legally only allowed in very limited circumstances and are very unusual in primary schools).

The LEA must consult on its proposed admission arrangements each school year by 1 March and following consultation, decide on the arrangements by 15 April for intakes from September of the following year.

The LEA must send a written copy of their proposed admission arrangements to the other admission authorities they have to consult, inviting their views and comments. Once it has decided on its arrangements – having considered any consultation responses – it must write to all the other admission authorities it consulted. If you, or anyone else consulted about the admission arrangements, have any objections, you can raise them at the local Admissions Forum or to the School's Adjudicator. You have to do this within six weeks of the date of publication of the

If yours is a foundation or voluntary aided primary school, or another primary school for which the governing body is the admission authority for the school, you must similarly consult the LEA and other admission authorities in the relevant area. Before determining your admission arrangements, you must also consult any neighbouring LEA, if part of that LEA's area is within 3.2 km of the school's main entrance. Then you send a copy of the arrangements to all the admission authorities consulted.

arrangements. Local Admissions Forums have been set up so that all admission authorities in an area can consider how local arrangements can best meet the needs of parents and children. They also look at how the admission arrangements interrelate with other issues such as planning, local population changes and provision for children with special needs or challenging behaviour.

School admission arrangements

Parents of children between the ages of 5 and 16 must see that their children receive suitable full-time education. The LEA is responsible for making sure that parents carry out this duty and that there are sufficient school places for the children in their area. Children have to attend school from the term immediately after their fifth birthday. One of the key aims of the School Admissions Code of Practice is that school admission arrangements should work for the benefit of all parents and children in an area. The arrangements should be as simple as possible for parents to use and help them make the best decisions on the school for their child. Parents applying for a school place for their child need

- local admission arrangements that are clear and give every child a fair chance of a satisfactory school place
- full information for an informed choice
- local admission procedures that are well coordinated and easy to follow, maximising the opportunity of having their school preference met
- an effective statutory right of appeal if dissatisfied.

Oversubscription is the most common reason why parental preference can't be met

You have to publish information about your school in the school prospectus or brochure and the LEA must publish information about admission arrangements for yours and all the other maintained mainstream schools in its area. According to government guidelines, information is most helpful when it

- offers clear guidance in plain English and in commonly used community languages to guide parents through the procedure
- sets out clearly the timescale for each stage of the admissions process, particularly the deadline for receipt of applications
- explains briefly each school's admission policy and oversubscription criteria and how they are applied and, if necessary, whether any extra information in support of application is required
- provides relevant information on admission arrangements for disabled children

If the governing body is the admission authority for your school, you may delegate the role of determining applications for places to a committee of which the headteacher must be a member. You can't, however, delegate it to any individual.

- makes clear when parents will know whether or not their applications have been successful and how to take up their statutory right of appeal
- gives a name and details of a contact point for further information
- gives the number of applicants who were successful in previous years, whether and to what extent the school was oversubscribed in the past and the criteria under which children were accepted
- explains what is expected from parents and what the parents can expect from the school and the LEA at each stage.

(Based on DfEE, 1999a, Section 3.6)

The Education (School Information) (England) (Amendment) Regulations 1999 require that parents are provided with, as a minimum, the name and address of the school, contact details, school's classification, summary of admissions policy including arrangements for disabled children and, where relevant, a statement of religious affiliation.

The LEA has a duty to make arrangements for parents to express a preference as to which school they would like their child to attend and to give reasons for their preference. The Rotherham Judgement of 1997 (see DfEE, 1999a, Section 5.5) established that LEAs must consider the views of parents who have expressed a preference ahead of those who haven't expressed any preference.

Oversubscription criteria

When you publish your admission arrangements you must include the oversubscription criteria that will be used to allocate places if there are more applicants than places available at a particular school. The criteria chosen may make it necessary for the LEA to provide more information to help parental choice. For instance, where distance from the school or catchment areas is used, admission authorities should consider whether a map of the area should be made available to parents. The Greenwich Judgement of 1989 (see DfEE, 1999a, Section 5.4) established that LEAs could not give priority to applicants living in the authority's administrative area. However, the Rotherham Judgement of 1997 confirmed that there is nothing unlawful in the principle of admission authorities operating catchment areas as part of oversubscription criteria and thereby giving priority to local children.

Oversubscription is the most common reason why parental preference can't be met. All maintained schools have to have a *standard number* for each of the relevant age groups – that is, the age groups in which children are normally admitted to the school. The standard number is the minimum number of children a school must admit if sufficient applications for places are received. As admissions authority, the LEA has a duty to keep standard numbers under review, bearing in mind the school's capacity. If the number of children a school can accommodate either reduces or increases, the LEA (or the governing body for foundation or voluntary aided schools) can apply to the School Organisation Committee, which each LEA must establish, for an appropriate variation to the set standard number. The procedures, which must be followed, are set out in DfEE Circular 9/99 (DfEE, 1999c).

The LEA must not fix an admission number for a relevant age group that is lower than the standard number. But it can set a higher admission number, provided it's compatible with the duty to comply with the infant class size limit of 30 children. Once an admission number has been set, children should not be admitted above the published admission number (PAN) unless exceptional circumstances apply.

In the case of oversubscription the LEA must apply the oversubscription criteria in its published admission policy in order to decide which parents' preferences it should meet. Frequently used and acceptable criteria include sibling links, distance from the school, medical or social grounds, accessibility by public transport, or possibly, as in the case of schools supported by religious foundations, preference to members of a particular faith or denomination.

Although your governing body might not be the admissions authority for your school, you still need to be familiar with the admission arrangements and how they are applied. As well as taking part in the regular consultations you should also be ready to make representations to the LEA if a change in circumstances means that the school is able to take fewer or more children.

Appeals

Parents who are refused a school place have the right to appeal to an independent panel set up by the admissions authority. In the case of community schools this duty falls on the LEA, even when the governing body is the admissions authority. The appeals panel is independent of the LEA and governing body that made the original admission decision and, as governor of the school, you can't be a member.

Although including medical grounds in oversubscription criteria might be interpreted as meaning a degree of disability discrimination, in a sense this may be viewed as positive discrimination. Some schools have specialist departments such as a hearing-impaired unit or attached unit for children with autism. In the case of most mainstream schools, children who have particular social and/or medical needs often have reasonable grounds for appeal if they are not offered a place at the school of their choice. In most cases the parents will have shown a preference for a particular school bearing their child's needs in mind. Thus appeals panels will tend to find in their favour. In some areas there may be particular schools that have better facilities for access for disabled children than others. You may find it sensible to reflect these issues in your oversubscription criteria.

Appeals panels, established under the terms of the School Standards and Framework Act of 1998, are

- entirely independent of LEAs and governing bodies involved in making the original admissions decision
- limited to five members
- required to operate with regard to guidance in the statutory admission appeals Code of Practice.

Where a panel finds in favour of the parent, the decision is binding.

Parents are entitled to apply for a place for their child at more than one school. They are equally entitled to make an appeal in respect of each unsuccessful application or regarding the school they have been allocated for their child. This right also applies at other than the normal times of entry to a school. The admission appeals Code of Practice is intended to be as open, fair and effective as possible.

It's a good idea for you to monitor school admissions, refusals of places and appeals so that you can keep a check on whether your admissions process is fair and offers equal opportunities to all children.

Attainment and progress

One of your duties as a governor is to make sure that your school provides the best possible education. As part of this responsibility and to help the school focus attention on improving its overall performance, you have to set and publish challenging targets for children's achievement.

In doing this your key roles are

- providing a strategic view
- acting as a 'critical friend'
- ensuring accountability.

Chapter 3, 'School improvement', covers this process and your role in it in detail.

Special educational needs (SEN)

Definition

Children are considered to have special educational needs if they have a learning difficulty that calls for special educational provision to be made for them. Section 312 of the Education Act 1996 defines children to have a learning difficulty if they

- have a significantly greater difficulty in learning than the majority of children of the same age
- have a disability that prevents or hinders them from making use of educational facilities of a kind generally provided for children of the same age in schools within the area of the local education authority
- are under compulsory school age and fall within the definitions above or would do so if special educational provision was not made for them.

Children with SEN all have difficulties that make it much harder for them to learn in the same way as most children of the same age

The definition includes those with a range of underlying factors such as cognitive, physical or sensory difficulties, emotional and behavioural difficulties or difficulties with speech and language or social interaction. Such children may need additional or different help from that given to other children of the same age. Children must not be regarded as having a learning difficulty solely because the language or form of language of their home is different from the language in which they will be taught.

Inclusion

The revised SEN Code of Practice (DfES, 2001a) emphasises the policy of developing a more inclusive education system. *Inclusion* is the practice of including all children together in a setting so that a child with SEN will remain, wherever possible, in a mainstream setting for their education – with any relevant and appropriate support they may require. A child with SEN should be offered full access to a broad, balanced and relevant education, including appropriate access to the National Curriculum. The idea is that, through inclusion, children with SEN will develop a higher self-esteem and positive attitude towards learning.

A further aim of inclusion is that children who don't have special educational needs will learn to view all people, including those with special needs or disabilities, as valued members of society both in school and in the wider world. Unless parents indicate that they don't want their child to be educated in a mainstream school, LEAs must make sure that provision is made in a mainstream school unless that would be incompatible with the efficient education of other children.

Provision

The SEN Code of Practice describes a graduated approach as a model of action and intervention in schools to help children who have SEN. The approach recognises that there is a continuum of SEN and increasing specialist expertise may be needed depending on the difficulties that a child may be experiencing. Two particular stages are identified – School Action and School Action Plus – which cover the needs of the majority of children.

School Action

When staff identify that a child has SEN, the class teacher devises interventions additional to or different from those provided as part of the school's usual differentiated curriculum. The class teacher remains responsible for working with the child on a daily basis and for planning and delivering an individualised programme, for which an individual education plan (IEP) will usually be devised. The SEN coordinator may help in planning future interventions for the child in discussion with colleagues and may be involved in monitoring and reviewing the action.

School Action Plus

This is the stage when the class teacher and SEN coordinator, in consultation with parents, ask for help from external services. Advice or support may be provided from outside agencies and additional or different strategies from those at School Action are put into place, for which an individual

education plan is devised. The SEN coordinator takes the lead in any further assessment of the child, planning future interventions for the child in discussion with colleagues and for monitoring and reviewing the action taken.

Individual education plans

Strategies employed to help a child with SEN to progress should be recorded in an IEP. The IEP is a planning, teaching and reviewing tool, which should underpin the process of planning intervention for the individual child with SEN. An IEP will include information about

- the short-term targets set for or by the child
- the teaching strategies to be used
- the provision to be put in place
- when the plan is to be reviewed
- success and/or exit criteria
- outcomes (to be recorded when the IEP is reviewed).

The IEP should only record anything that is additional to or different from the differentiated curriculum plan, which is in place as part of provision for all children. The IEP should focus on three or four individual targets chosen from those relating to the key areas of communication, literacy, maths, and behaviour and social skills, that match the child's needs.

The class teacher and/or the SEN coordinator should discuss the IEP with the child and the parents and ideally involve the child in deciding and agreeing the targets. IEPs should be reviewed at least twice a year, although they may be reviewed termly and possibly more frequently for some children. Reviews are usually arranged by the SEN coordinator.

Statements

The special educational needs of most children should be met effectively through School Action and School Action Plus without the LEA needing to be heavily involved. In a very small number of cases the LEA will need to make a statutory assessment of special educational needs and then consider whether or not to issue a 'statement' of special educational needs.

Statutory assessment involves consideration by the LEA, working cooperatively with parents, the child's school and, as appropriate, other agencies, as to whether a statement of the child's special educational needs is necessary. Statutory assessment itself will not always lead to a statement, as the information gathered during an assessment may indicate ways in which the school can meet the child's needs. A request for an assessment may be made by the child's school or setting, by the child's parents or through referral by another agency.

Statements of special educational needs must follow the format set out in the 2002 SEN Code of Practice and should always contain the following prescribed information.

Part 1 Introduction (name, address, date of birth, home language, religion, parents' details).

Part 2 Special Educational Needs (describing the child's current difficulties).

Part 3 Special Educational Provision (including objectives and monitoring arrangements and what additional or different provision must be made).

Part 4 Placement (which must be left blank when a proposed statement is issued).

Part 5 Non-Educational Needs (such as special therapy, specialist medical intervention, respite care, mobility training, travel provision).

Part 6 Non-Educational Provision (to meet the needs identified in Part 5).

All the advice obtained and taken into consideration during the assessment process must be attached as appendices to the statement. This will include parental evidence, educational, medical, psychological and social services advice, plus any other advice such as the views of the child.

The LEA must consult the governing body of a school before naming it in Part 4 of a statement, and consultation should take place before it makes the final decision. You will need to know if any particular facilities, equipment, staffing arrangements or curriculum modifications will be needed and the provisions that are proposed to assist the placement in practical and curricular terms. Where a maintained school is named in a statement, the governing body must admit the child to the school.

All statements must be reviewed at least annually. At a review the parents, the child, the LEA, the school – and all the other professionals involved – consider the progress the child has made over the last 12 months. They also decide whether any amendments need to be made to the description of the child's needs or to the special educational provision specified in the statement. Each term the LEA sends the headteacher a list of annual reviews . The head, or perhaps the SEN coordinator, then initiates the review process.

SEN governor checklist

- ❑ Do you have an overview of your school's work with children who have special educational needs?
- ❑ Are you familiar with the SEN Code of Practice?
- ❑ Is your school making the necessary special arrangements for children who have special educational needs?
- ❑ Do you know your LEA's policy on providing any extra funding for the teaching and support of children with statements and children who do not have statements but who need support from outside the school?
- ❑ Who is your school's responsible person – the person who is responsible for making all staff who are likely to teach a child with SEN aware of their needs?
- ❑ Are all the teachers at your school aware of the importance of identifying children who have special educational needs and providing appropriate teaching?
- ❑ What steps does your school take to identify SEN early?
- ❑ Have any variances to the National Curriculum, where appropriate, been agreed?
- ❑ Is your school providing equal access to children including those with disabilities and special educational needs?
- ❑ Do children with special needs join in the everyday activities of your school as far as is practical?
- ❑ Who is your school's SEN coordinator?
- ❑ Is your SEN coordinator's timetable appropriate in light of the 2002 Code of Practice and resources available?
- ❑ Are the staffing and funding arrangements for SEN appropriate?
- ❑ Has your school set targets for children with SEN at Key Stage 2?
- ❑ How is your school's work in SEN monitored – is there quality provision?
- ❑ Are your school's SEN policies freely available to parents?
- ❑ Does your annual governor's report to parents include a section about the provision for SEN in your school. Is it readable and attractive? Is the language appropriate for all parents?
- ❑ How are the views of children who have SEN and their parents sought and taken into consideration?
- ❑ How is your school developing knowledge and securing training, advice and support for staff working in SEN?
- ❑ When is your school SEN policy due to be reviewed and updated?

SEN coordinator

Every school should have an SEN coordinator. The SEN coordinator, in collaboration with the headteacher and the governing body, plays a key role in determining the strategic development of the SEN policy and provision in the school in order to raise achievement of children with special educational needs. The SEN coordinator takes day-to-day responsibility for the operation of the SEN policy and coordination of the provision made for individual children with SEN, working closely with staff, parents/carers and other agencies. The SEN coordinator also provides related professional advice to colleagues with the aim of securing high-quality teaching for children with SEN. In order to fulfil these duties, sufficient time needs to be allocated for the SEN coordinator to use their expertise effectively.

The duties of the governing body

The governing body has important statutory duties towards children with special educational needs. These include making sure that the necessary provision is made for these children and that your school takes account of the SEN Code of Practice.

In doing this, you should, with the headteacher, agree the school's SEN policy and the school's approach to meeting the special educational needs of children with and without statements. You should oversee the school's work and set up appropriate staffing and funding arrangements. You should review the policy and its effectiveness each year.

You have a duty to promote high standards relating to all children in the school, including those with SEN. Thus objectives for leadership, management, pupil achievement and progress and priorities in the school improvement or development plan should include objectives relating to SEN.

You must make sure that your school has a responsible person who makes sure that all those who are likely to teach a child with a statement of special educational needs are told about the statement. The responsible person is generally the headteacher, but may be the chair of governors or another governor appointed by the governing body to take this responsibility. When a statement of special educational needs is made, the LEA informs the responsible person in a school. This person must then make sure that the child's special educational needs are made known to all those who will teach him or her.

You must see that children with special educational needs are encouraged to join in the activities of the school together with children who do not have special educational needs so far as is reasonably practical. Your annual report to parents must include information on the implementation of the school's policy for children with special educational needs and any changes to the policy during the last year.

You are responsible for ensuring that parents are informed if their child has special educational needs for which special provision is being made. You will usually delegate this to the headteacher, who will decide how to involve other members of staff, as appropriate, in informing parents and encouraging their partnership.

You might want to appoint a governor or committee to have a specific oversight of the school's arrangements and provision for meeting special educational needs. See the 'SEN governor checklist' on page 68.

Behaviour and discipline

Behaviour and discipline policy

The management of discipline in schools is very important for the welfare of both children and staff and to promote a positive teaching, learning and social environment. Your school has to have a behaviour and discipline policy which makes clear

- the boundaries of what is acceptable behaviour
- the hierarchy of sanctions to tackle unacceptable behaviour
- arrangements for consistent and fair application of sanctions
- a linked system of rewards for good behaviour.

See the table below.

Your behaviour and discipline policy should promote respect for others, intolerance of all forms of bullying and harassment, the importance of self-discipline, proper regard for authority and the difference between right and wrong. Under the School Standards and Framework Act 1998, the headteacher is responsible for promoting good behaviour and discipline in line with the written statement of general principles prepared by the governing body. While you may provide guidance and put forward the governing body's views, which must be taken into account, the headteacher has responsibility for putting principles into practice and for dealing with individual cases. The headteacher must also publicise the school behaviour and discipline policy at least once a year to children, parents and staff. The policy should be available in relevant languages, as appropriate, to meet the requirement to publicise it to all parents. See 'Template for a behaviour and discipline policy' on page 70.

'Bullying can be defined as deliberately hurtful behaviour, repeated over a period of time, where it is difficult for those being bullied to defend themselves.' (a–z Bullying, www.dfes.gov.uk)

Behaviour and discipline – roles and responsibilities

Responsibility	Role	Task
Behaviour/discipline policy	Governing body	Consult with headteacher, parents and possibly children
Maintaining high standards of discipline	Headteacher	Governors to discuss feedback from headteacher's report to governors Feedback from governor visits to the school
Discipline committee	Governing body	Governors to agree members of this committee – perhaps at the first meeting each academic year
Exclusions	Headteacher	The headteacher must inform the discipline committee of exclusions of more than five days and immediately in the case of a permanent exclusion
Appeals panel	LEA	Governors may be represented at meetings of an appeals panel

Template for a behaviour and discipline policy

General philosophy

The philosophy of the behaviour and discipline policy of the school may come from a code of conduct drawn up by children and staff, eg. 'treat everyone with kindness and respect, be careful with others' property, always walk quietly and sensibly round the school'. Rules may be included here or listed separately.

Aims of the policy

These might be to develop a moral framework within which initiative, responsibility and sound relationships can flourish. Aims might cover areas such as morals, self and environment.

Objectives

For instance, for children to show or develop self-confidence, self-control, consideration for others.

Implementation

How the policy is implemented – for instance, the behaviour and responsibility of all staff.

Children

This might describe how achievements – academic or otherwise – are recognised and rewarded.

Unacceptable behaviour

This might be clearly listed and described, as appropriate. It may be useful to consider different situations such as in the classroom, in assembly, in the playground.

Sanctions

This section would include a clear list of agreed sanctions for unacceptable behaviour – for instance, the use of detention – and how they will be applied.

Parents

This might include the school's approach to encouraging good communication and parental partnership.

Other agencies

This section might refer to how the school develops positive involvement with other agencies such as the police.

Care of school premises and sites

Some schools may wish to make particular references to the environment – for instance, about safe (supervised only) use of fixed playground equipment.

Bullying

The headteacher has a legal duty to draw up procedures to prevent bullying among children and to bring these procedures to the attention of staff, parents and children. Such procedures should be well publicised throughout the school. Effective anti-bullying strategies should normally form part of the school's behaviour and discipline policy.

Three main types of bullying are

- *physical* (eg. hitting, kicking, theft)
- *verbal* (eg. name-calling, racist remarks)
- *indirect* (eg. spreading rumours, excluding someone from social groups).

Being bullied in whatever form is emotionally distressing and can badly affect school achievement, lead to lateness or non-attendance and cause ill health. School staff should be alert to signs of bullying and should be seen to act promptly and firmly against it in accordance with the school policy. Incidents should be properly documented, together with details of the action taken in order to have a record in the case of subsequent incidents or enquiries. The DfES provides further guidance for schools, which also complies with the Human Rights Act 1998 (DfES, 2001b, Annex 5).

The role of the governing body

You must set the framework of a school's behaviour and discipline policy through a written statement of general principles that takes account of the needs of all children, including any with special educational needs. The statement should be reviewed regularly and should cover

- the ethos of the school, its values and the boundaries of acceptable behaviour
- the school's moral code
- positive and constructive rules of conduct
- the rewards and punishments to be fairly and consistently applied.

It's good practice for you to consult the headteacher and parents of children before making or revising the statement, in order to take account of their views. Consultation with parents could be at your annual meeting for parents, at a specially convened meeting or in writing.

The governing body should oversee the headteacher's maintenance of discipline at the school in line with their policies. To do this you will need information – probably through the headteacher's report – about such things as any temporary/permanent exclusions. You can also gather valuable information and impressions by visiting the school during the working day. Nevertheless, it's important to remember that the head has day-to-day responsibility for discipline. You should advise the head of your views on specific measures for promoting good behaviour and you have a general duty to make sure that the school follows policies to promote good behaviour and discipline. You should regularly review your school's behaviour and discipline policy, and the school anti-bullying policy if this is a separate document.

Implementation

The DfES has outlined various principles of good practice that you may wish to draw on.

Setting good habits early – to help children establish regular punctual attendance and good behaviour from the start, involving parents in the process.

Early intervention – prompt intervention is needed where there is poor behaviour or unexplained absence to clarify and emphasise expectations.

Rewarding achievements – positive recognition of individual children, class or group achievements in good attendance and behaviour, such as through mentions in assemblies, certificates or prizes.

Supporting behaviour management – using behaviour management techniques such as assertive discipline and various activities such as circletime in order to improve and maintain high standards of behaviour.

Identifying underlying causes – poor behaviour may sometimes be linked to a child's problems in understanding lessons, and therefore require additional literacy or numeracy support to address them effectively.

Study support – many activities such as homework clubs and thinking-skills groups help to reinforce school work. Parents might be invited to attend a session about a certain area of the curriculum, which may help them support their own children with school work and encourage a channel of communication with the school.

Commitment to equal opportunities – parents and children should know that the school has an equal opportunities policy and is committed to equality of opportunity for all children.

(Based on a–z Pupil Discipline Policy, on www.dfes.gov.uk)

Involving children can help to reinforce school behaviour policies by active involvement in such things as anti-bullying policies. Many schools encourage children to contribute their ideas through a school council and in class discussions. All schools should encourage parents to support good attendance and behaviour through home–school agreements, parents' evenings and newsletters.

You can take an active role in all this by, for example, asking for feedback from staff, having a presentation or discussion at a governor's meeting and sending a questionnaire to parents.

> The organisation of policies, the school's environment and overall ethos can all have a strong influence on children's behaviour. As the role of the governing body can be central to influencing the ethos of the school, you should take a positive lead in establishing principles for the school's policy on behaviour and discipline. You can do this by taking a keen interest in what standards of behaviour and discipline are evident when you visit the school and as documented in the headteacher's report. You can also encourage staff to have high expectations, and support good practice through enquiring about and, where appropriate approving, ongoing staff development and training.

Lunchtime supervision

The management of children's behaviour at lunchtime is an important priority in many schools. For most children this is an important time of the day when they have an opportunity to develop their social skills. Critically, it is also a time when children can feel at risk of intimidation and bullying. The responsibilities of lunchtime supervisors should involve providing an organised and structured lunchtime and, through promoting positive behaviour, providing a safe and secure environment for all children.

As a governor you should recognise the need for supervisors to have the opportunity to develop their knowledge and expertise, particularly in the area of behaviour management. Lunchtime supervisors need to be fully aware of, and able to maintain discipline in line with, the school's behaviour and discipline policy. You may need to consider the implications for resources and the provision of adequate training for staff supervising children at lunchtimes. To get a better understanding of the situation, it's useful to plan a visit that coincides with lunchtime break and wander round the dining hall and playground.

Detention

Detention at the end of a school session is one of the sanctions schools can use against bad behaviour. However, there are certain conditions that must be satisfied.

- It must be made known to all parents and children in the school's behaviour and discipline policy that detention may be used as a disciplinary sanction.
- The detention must be imposed by the headteacher or by a member of staff authorised by the headteacher.
- The detention must be reasonable and proportionate to the offence.
- At least 24 hours' written notice must be given to the parents of a child concerned before the detention takes place.

(Based on a – z Detention, www.dfes.gov.uk)

A notice to parents should inform them that their child has been given a detention, why the detention was given and details of the detention arrangements – when, where and for how long the child will have to remain at school. Parents who have objections to a detention may present any relevant facts for the headteacher to take into account. The headteacher should also take into account

- the age of the child
- any special educational needs the child may have
- any relevant religious requirements
- if arrangements have to be made for the child to travel home, whether suitable alternative arrangements can reasonably be made.

A parent concerned about either the principle of detention or how it's used can raise these concerns with the headteacher or governing body, or both, under the school's normal complaints procedure. However, there will usually not be time to consider a specific complaint until after the detention has taken place. Even then, there is no right of appeal and you have no power to overturn a decision even if you are able to consider a complaint before the detention takes place.

Use of force to restrain children

It's a good idea to include in your behaviour and discipline policy something about the use of force to control or restrain children. This should make it clear to staff, parents and children what is

acceptable and what isn't. Corporal punishment is forbidden but the Education Act 1996 allows teachers to use reasonable force to prevent a child from

- committing a criminal offence
- injuring themselves or others
- damaging property
- acting in a way that is counter to maintaining good order and discipline in the school.

The Act doesn't cover more extreme cases, such as action in self-defence or in an emergency, when it might be considered reasonable for someone to use a degree of force. Staff other than teachers and volunteer helpers are also able to use force if necessary, provided they have been authorised by the headteacher to have control or charge of children. Such staff might include teaching assistants, midday supervisors and support staff. The headteacher might find it helpful to provide training or guidance to make sure that everyone is clear on the policy. You could reasonably expect the head to keep detailed and up-to-date records of any incidents where force or restraint is used. It's advisable that parents are informed of such an incident and for staff to allow an opportunity to discuss it.

Exclusion

The Schools Standards and Framework Act 1998 governs the exclusion of children from maintained schools. Exclusion on disciplinary grounds may fall into two categories – fixed-period exclusion and permanent exclusion.

Children may also be excluded from the school premises for the duration of the lunchtime break between the morning and the afternoon sessions. Government guidance states that a decision to exclude a child should be taken only

- in response to serious breaches of a school's discipline policy
- if allowing the child to remain in school would seriously harm the education or welfare of the child or others in the school.

(DfES, 2001b, Chapter 13, section 7)

In most cases, before excluding a child a range of alternative strategies, which might include such things as a pastoral support programme (PSP), should have been tried. For children with a statement of special educational needs, revision of the statement might be a preferable alternative to exclusion.

The discipline committee

The governing body has no power to exclude a child – it's the decision of the headteacher. Your role is to review the headteacher's exclusion decisions. You are required to set up a discipline committee made up of three to five governors (not to include the headteacher), to review the use of exclusion within the school (DfEE, 2000, Annex D p52; DfES, 2001b, Chapter 13, para 13). The committee will need to have a clerk to provide advice on the exclusions process and to deal with administration.

The headteacher has to notify the discipline committee and the LEA immediately about any permanent exclusion and any exclusion that would mean a child missing more than five school days in a term. This information must include

- the child's name
- the length of the exclusion
- the reasons
- the child's age, gender, ethnicity and whether they have special educational needs (with or without a statement)
- whether they are looked after by the local authority.

The governing body has no power to exclude a child – it is the decision of the headteacher

> If you have a connection to a particular child or the incident that could affect your ability to act impartially, you shouldn't serve at that hearing.

When you are told about an exclusion, the clerk to the discipline committee arranges a meeting. If it's an exclusion of between 6 and 15 school days, the meeting has to be held some time between the 6th and the 50th day after it began. If the exclusion is for more than 15 days, the meeting should be held between 6 and 15 days of the notice being received from the headteacher.

The clerk invites the parent (who can be accompanied by a friend or legal representative) and the LEA to the meeting. The excluded child can, normally, also attend to present his or her case if so desired. The clerk also asks for any written statements to be submitted before the meeting takes place. The clerk then distributes these – making sure that children's identities are not revealed – together with a list of those who will be attending.

At the meeting you have to

- consider statements from parents and the LEA
- consider whether the headteacher has done enough to improve the child's behaviour and whether anything else could be done instead of excluding them

- in a case of permanent exclusion, satisfy yourself that every possible strategy has been tried and has failed
- order direct reinstatement if the headteacher has not used exclusion in line with the guidance in Section 6 of DfEE Circular 10/99 (DfEE, 2000).

If you decide that a child should be reinstated, you must notify the headteacher, who has a duty to comply with this decision. You must also inform the parents and the LEA of your decision.

If you decide that a child shouldn't be reinstated, you must similarly inform the headteacher, parents and LEA. In the case of a permanent exclusion, you must notify the parents in writing within one school day of the hearing, giving the reasons for your decision. This letter must also advise the parents of their right to appeal against the decision, telling them who to contact, the last day for lodging an appeal, and that they should set out the grounds of appeal.

As a governor you won't be directly involved in child protection cases ... Your role is more concerned with making sure that procedures are in place

The appeal panel

Where the discipline committee has upheld a permanent exclusion, the parents may appeal against your decision, in which case the LEA must establish an appeal panel, again consisting of three to five members. This panel must allow you, the headteacher and the LEA to make written representations, and allow the headteacher, a member of the discipline committee and an officer of the LEA to attend and make oral representations. The panel must also allow the discipline committee to be legally represented. The parents are also invited to attend, along with a legal or other representative. The panel must give its decision in writing to the parties concerned, including the governing body, by the end of the second day after the conclusion of the panel hearing. The decision of the panel is binding on everyone.

Statutory funding for any child follows the pupil – and if a child is permanently excluded, any amount to be transferred to the new education provider is calculated in accordance with the formula laid down in regulations made under the School Standards and Framework Act 1998.

Child protection

Everyone working in your school can contribute to the safeguarding of children and to child protection processes. The Children Act 1989 gives every child the right to protection from abuse and exploitation and the right to have enquiries made to safeguard their welfare. Your school has a pastoral responsibility towards its children and can play a part in the prevention of abuse and neglect, through your own policies and procedures, and through the curriculum.

Categories of abuse

Certain categories of abuse are recognised for the purposes of the child protection register, which is a register of children at risk of abuse and is maintained by the local social services department. These categories are

- neglect
- physical injury
- sexual abuse
- emotional abuse.

Responsibilities

Through their day-to-day contact with children and direct work with families, school staff have a crucial role to play in noticing possible abuse or neglect. Your school must develop a child protection policy that includes procedures for dealing with suspected cases of child abuse. It's very important that all staff understand that the responsibility for investigating such cases lies with other agencies. DfEE Circular 10/95 *Protecting Children from Abuse: The Role of the Education Service* (DfEE, 1995) outlines guidance to the education service on its role in helping to protect children from abuse. Staff should be alert to signs of abuse and be fully aware of the school's child protection procedures. Your school must have a designated teacher (usually the headteacher or another senior teacher) who is appropriately trained and responsible for coordinating actions within the school and for liaising with other agencies including the Area Child Protection Committee (ACPC).

As a governor you won't be directly involved in child protection cases. Even when you are aware that something is being investigated you won't be given any details and anything you do know is strictly confidential. Your role is more concerned with making sure that procedures are in place. You may occasionally be asked to consider staffing implications and funding for specific training. If you are the nominated governor you might report back to the governing body about staff training and any discussions concerning procedures with the designated teacher – but such discussions and reports should always be general rather than about specific details.

The designated teacher has specific responsibility for the coordination of child protection procedures within the school and for liaison with social services and other agencies. The school must make sure that all staff are aware who the designated teacher is. It can do this through staff induction information and by naming the designated teacher on the school's child protection policy. All cases of suspected abuse should be reported to this person in the first instance.

You need to make sure that the school does have a child protection policy in place and that this has been approved by the full governing body. The headteacher should then make sure that parents are aware of the policy. In addition to a designated member of staff, it's good practice for you to nominate a governor who is responsible for liaising with the headteacher and designated teacher over child protection issues. The nominated governor would also have responsibility for the oversight of procedures relating to allegations against the headteacher.

Procedure

The DfES (a–z Child Protection, on www.dfes.gov.uk) has outlined the following child protection procedure.

- When a teacher or other member of staff suspects abuse or hears a sustainable allegation they should report the information to the designated teacher.
- The designated teacher should then refer the case to or discuss it with social services and/or the police according to the procedures established by the local Area Child Protection Committee and by the LEA.
- If the designated teacher is unsure about whether the case should be formally referred, they can seek advice and support from the local social services department, the NSPCC or the LEA child protection coordinator.
- The designated teacher is responsible for liaising with and keeping the headteacher informed.
- The designated teacher should clarify how and by whom the parents and the child will be told that a referral has been made.
- The designated teacher will want to be kept informed about discussions between the statutory agencies, which will decide whether and how to investigate, and the designated teacher or another member of staff should be prepared to contribute to such discussions.

Inter-agency cooperation

As efficient transfer of information is essential, your school should contribute to a coordinated approach to child protection by developing effective liaison with other agencies and support services. The designated teacher should establish good working relationships with colleagues from other agencies, especially the local social services department. The social services department should notify the school if a child has been placed on, or removed from, the child protection register or when a child whose name is on the register starts at the school.

The school should monitor children whose names are on the child protection register in line with what has been agreed in the child protection plan and the designated teacher should report any further concerns to the social services department. School staff may need to be released from normal duties for essential meetings, to prepare written reports or to attend case conferences as required.

Allegations against members of staff

Where an allegation is made against a teacher, there should be an urgent initial consideration by the headteacher, in consultation with child protection agencies, of whether or not there is sufficient substance in an allegation to warrant an investigation. Unless there is an objection by the child protection agency concerned, the headteacher should inform the chair of the governing body. If a teacher is suspended, the head should inform the chair of governors in writing. The head should report to the governing body that a teacher has been suspended pending investigation. It is inadvisable for the head to provide you with more than the minimum information necessary, as this would prejudice your impartiality in any subsequent hearing or appeal in disciplinary proceedings.

This is a very complex area regarding the law, conduct of investigations, inter-agency involvement and procedures. You will want to contact your Area Child Protection Committee, who will advise you on current procedures.

In a case in which the headteacher is accused, you should certainly obtain appropriate current advice. You may need to consider carefully whether suspension of the headteacher is the appropriate course of action. Bearing in mind that although suspension on full pay is in law a 'neutral act' (DfEE, 1995), it's bound to be distressing for the accused person and disruptive for the school. You should also take into account the seriousness and plausibility of the allegation, the risk of harm to the child concerned or to other children and the possibilities of tampering with evidence.

Promoting regular school attendance is a key factor in raising educational standards

Importance of child protection

All schools should create and maintain a safe environment for children and should be able to manage situations where there are child welfare concerns. Children can be helped to understand what is and what is not acceptable behaviour towards them. They can be taught about staying safe from harm, and how to speak up if they have worries or concerns. The curriculum can play a useful preventative role in developing awareness and preparing children for their future responsibilities as adults, parents and citizens.

Attendance

All children of compulsory school age (5–16 years) should receive suitable education, either by regular attendance at school or otherwise. If a child is registered at a school, parents have the primary responsibility for ensuring that their child attends regularly. If their child doesn't attend, they can be prosecuted. LEAs are responsible in law for making sure that children attend school and most LEAs employ education welfare officers (EWOs) to work with schools and families to promote regular attendance.

Promoting regular school attendance is a key factor in raising educational standards and is also important in reducing wider social problems associated with social exclusion. Children who fail to attend regularly, experience increasing educational disadvantage at school and impaired prospects later in life. They may be at higher risk of abuse and drifting into anti-social and criminal behaviour.

Registers

The governing body is responsible for making sure that two types of register are kept – one for admissions and one for attendance. Your school has to take an attendance register twice a day, at the start of each morning session and once during each afternoon session. In its registers the school

has to identify whether children are present, involved in an approved educational activity such as a school trip, or are absent. Registers are important documents and must be kept in a safe place as they may be needed for use in legal proceedings. They are often the only record of who is on site in the event of an emergency such as a fire.

The school may keep registers handwritten in ink or on computer. In either case, the original entry in the register and any subsequent correction must be clearly distinguishable. If the school uses a computer for attendance registration, staff must print the register at least once a month. At the end of each school year, sheets must be bound into annual volumes and, like manual registers, must be kept for three years from the last date of entry. The governing body, which is legally responsible for the attendance register, must register with the Data Protection Registrar under the Data Protection Act 1998. (Contact the Office of the Data Protection Commissioner, Wycliffe House, Water Lane, Wilmslow, Cheshire SK9 5AF. Tel: 01625 545700, www.dataprotection.gov.uk.)

Definitions of absence

If a child of compulsory school age is absent from school, the register must show whether the absence was authorised or unauthorised.

Authorised absence is where the school has either given approval in advance for a child to be absent, or has accepted an explanation offered afterwards as satisfactory justification for absence (eg. illness). Such absence, then, has permission from a teacher or other authorised representative of the school.

Unauthorised absence is absence without permission from a teacher or other representative of the school. This includes all unexplained or unjustified absences.

Parents may not authorise absence – only the school can do this. The school may authorise any absence but inappropriate use of this authority can be just as damaging to a child's education as unauthorised absence. Since all absences are to be treated as unauthorised unless and until there is an agreed satisfactory explanation, it's clearly important that the school has procedures, which it applies consistently, for chasing up explanations and amending registers. A table showing types of absence that schools may treat as authorised, with comprehensive remarks, is contained in DfEE Circular 10/99 (DfEE, 2000, Annex A). Such reasons include illness, medical and dental appointments, days of religious observance, family bereavement, exclusion and, in some instances, family holidays. Wherever possible, parents should be expected to give advance notice of absence.

The LEA is responsible for making sure that children of compulsory school age attend school regularly. At agreed intervals, you must give the LEA the name and address of every child who doesn't go to school regularly or who has had unauthorised absence for at least two weeks. You should also inform the LEA if a child is likely to be absent for more than four weeks on medical grounds, but in practice you are likely to delegate this responsibility to the headteacher.

Information

The school must include its absence rates in its prospectuses and in the annual governors' report. This is expressed in terms of the percentage of half-days (sessions) missed through authorised and unauthorised absence. You can expect the relevant information to be provided in the headteacher's regular reports. Similarly, reports on children's achievements sent to parents have to include information on the individual child's attendance record showing the number of times he or she was absent without permission (the number of missed sessions). Overall levels of children's absence are published every year in local comparative tables.

Strategies for improving attendance

You have a particular role with the headteacher in considering a whole-school approach to non-attendance, with particular reference to unauthorised absence.

If non-attendance is an issue that needs to be addressed in your school, you might devise a system of 'First Day Response'. This means that a member of staff (possibly from the school office) contacts parents on any day when a child is absent without explanation. This gives a clear message to children and parents that unauthorised absence is taken seriously and this strategy can lead to improved attendance. In addition, teaching staff may become involved through discussion with children and parents in order to overcome any possible underlying problems.

Other helpful approaches include the following.

- Using IT to improve monitoring of attendance. Trends and patterns can be more easily accessed by using a database and/or specially designed program.
- Raising the profile of attendance among parents through home–school agreements, parents' evenings, school newsletters or other communications.
- Regularly reminding parents of school procedures for notifying absence, and school policy on issues such as family holidays, which should not normally be during term time.

A model policy on providing access to educational records

Rationale

The governing body will make sure that a curricular record of each child is kept, which includes a formal record of academic achievements, other skills and abilities and progress in school. This record will include copies of individual reports. The chair of governors will check with the headteacher that such record-keeping is up to date on an annual basis (eg. July/September) and verify any change to the cost per sheet for charging. The chair will report back to the governors' meeting (another governor may be delegated these responsibilities).

Procedure

In the event of a parent or child making a written request to see the child's educational records, the governing body will allow the applicant (parent and/or child) to see these records within 15 days of receiving their written request. However, the Education (School Records) Regulations 1989 prevent the following information being disclosed.

- Material supplied by anyone other than employees of the school or LEA or the person requesting disclosure.
- Material whose disclosure would be likely to cause serious harm to the physical or mental health or the emotional condition of the child or someone else.
- Material concerning actual or suspected child abuse.
- Material that might reveal, or enable to be deduced, the identity of a person other than the child to whom the information relates.
- Reports by a school to juvenile courts.
- Statements of special educational needs.

While it is free of charge to see the records, the governing body will charge for copies of the records in order to cover the cost of this. Current charge per sheet is available from the school office/headteacher, to whom such charge should be paid before copies are given. Copies for other educational establishments are free.

Responsibility

The headteacher will be responsible for overseeing arrangements to reveal, transfer copy and change a child's record. Appeals concerning the headteacher's refusal to do any of these will be considered by the governing body following written request to the chair of governors.

If there is any doubt about whether and to what extent parents and children should be allowed access to pupil records, the headteacher or chair of governors will seek guidance from the Office of the Data Protection Commissioner, Wycliffe House, Water Lane, Wilmslow, Cheshire SK9 5AF (Tel: 01625 545700).

All records will be kept securely in a locked cabinet and personal information will be treated confidentially.

- Having a senior member of staff responsible for attendance.
- Having a governor who takes a particular interest in attendance figures and patterns.
- Group work with children who don't attend regularly, and with their parents.

Successful approaches to encouraging good attendance include informing and involving all staff, reviewing and tightening registration and lateness procedures, advising parents and children of appropriate procedures and expectations, and using reward systems such as certificates, badges and class awards. Although you are unlikely as a governor to be directly involved in any of this, you do have a part to play in monitoring the situation and encouraging appropriate action.

Educational records

In community schools, the headteacher must arrange for a curriculum record to be kept for each child and for this to be updated at least once a year. In foundation schools, responsibility rests with the governing body to make sure that this record is kept, although usually the headteacher or other staff carry out the actual tasks of keeping, updating and transferring records. This record is a formal record of academic achievements, progress in school, other skills and abilities, and it must include copies of school reports. There may be other records kept, such as details of behaviour and family background, but these aren't compulsory. This material, without the notes that teachers make for their own use, makes up the child's educational record. Guidance in the Education (Pupil Information) (England) Regulations 2000 consolidates legal requirements concerning the keeping, disclosure and transfer of a child's educational record. These take account of the Data Protection Act 1998 and strengthen the arrangements for the transfer of school records. See 'A model policy on providing access to educational records' on page 77.

In addition to the information that the school records for all children, the pupil record or profile for a child with special educational needs should include specific information. This includes details of the child's progress and behaviour from the school itself, from the child's early educational setting or a previous school, from the parents, and from health and social services. It should also include the child's own perception of any difficulties and how they might be addressed. The information collected should reveal the different perceptions of those concerned with the child, any immediate educational concerns and an overall picture of the child's strengths and weaknesses.

Disclosure

Children who submit written requests to see or receive a copy of their records should be allowed to do so unless exceptional circumstances apply or it is obvious that they do not understand what they are asking for. (Previously, children needed to have reached the age of 16.)

The headteacher must also allow parents to see or receive a copy of their child's educational records and in either instance records must be shown to children and parents free of charge. However, the Data Protection Act 1998 prevents disclosure of certain information (see 'Data protection' below). If there is any doubt about whether, and to what extent, children's records should be disclosed, the school should seek advice from the Data Protection Commissioner.

The headteacher must disclose a child's educational record within 15 school days of being asked for it in writing. Where a parent asks for a copy of a child's educational record, the headteacher may charge for it, but the charge, which must be set by the governing body, must not exceed the cost of supply. When agreeing the school's policy regarding educational records, you should decide whether a charge covering costs will be made and how this will be payable. In practice, if a charge is made you will probably delegate responsibility to the headteacher to organise to cover the cost of materials at a specified amount per sheet. Where a child asks for a copy of his or her educational record, any charge must be no higher than the cost of supply or the cost allowed under the Data Protection Act, whichever is the lesser. Information regarding this is available from the office of the Data Protection Commissioner.

The head must allow parents (and children if appropriate) who see a child's educational record to give notice that they wish to change or add to it if they consider that the record is not accurate. Any request for such a change should be attached to that record and become part of it. If a head refuses to reveal, copy or amend a child's educational record upon receiving a request, an appeal against their decision may be made through the courts.

Data protection

The Data Protection Act 1998 prevents disclosure of

- material supplied by anyone other than employees of the school or LEA or the person requesting disclosure
- material whose disclosure would be likely to cause serious harm to the physical or mental health or the emotional condition of the child or someone else
- material concerning actual or suspected child abuse
- material which might reveal, or enable to be deduced, the identity of a person other than the child to whom the information relates
- reports by a school to a juvenile court
- statements of special educational needs.

(Based on DfES, 2001b, Chapter 14, section 24)

However, the Data Protection Act does allow for this information to be transferred to another educational establishment.

Transfer of records

When a child transfers from one school to another, the headteacher must send the new school (maintained or independent) the completed statutory common transfer form. Normally this will be sent electronically using the Common Basic Data Set (CBDS). The head must also send all educational records relating to the child, including copies of their pupil reports.

The information must be sent within 15 school days of the child ceasing to be registered at the old school. Where the information cannot be transferred automatically because the destination

Outline of a home–school agreement

A home–school agreement explains the aims and values of your school. It spells out the responsibilities of the school and the responsibilities of parents and carers and what the school expects of its children. Each school must have a written home–school agreement, drawn up in consultation with the parents, outlining school policies in several areas including the following.

The standard of education the school will provide

This might include reference to meeting the needs of all children with a broad and balanced curriculum and what National Curriculum targets have been set.

The ethos of the school

This might consider how children relate to each other and staff and how the school relates to the community as a whole. Reference might be made to the school's aims for children's spiritual, moral, cultural and social development.

Regular, punctual attendance

Parents may be reminded of their statutory duties in making sure that their child attends school and that any absences must be explained in writing.

Discipline and behaviour

Rules and expectations for maintaining good standards of behaviour and discipline in school might be outlined.

Homework

This might give guidance on how much homework children of different ages should do. The amount recommended in government guidelines, in broad terms, is

- Years 1 and 2 – 1 hour a week reading, spelling, other literacy and number work
- Years 3 and 4 – 1.5 hours a week as above and with occasional assignments in other subjects
- Years 5 and 6 – 30 minutes a day literacy, numeracy and a wider range of other subjects.

The home–school agreement may just say that parents are expected to support the school's homework policy, without repeating details.

Communications

This might outline what information schools and parents will give to one another and information such as the timing of written reports and newsletters.

Complaints

The procedure or system whereby parents and carers are able to discuss any concerns or problems might be outlined.

Space should be left on the agreement for signatures and the headteacher may wish to sign on behalf of the school. The governing body must take reasonable steps to make sure that all registered parents sign the parental declaration, showing that they understand and accept the agreement. Children may also be invited to sign. However, refusal to sign an agreement should not result in adverse consequences for a child or parent and can't be made a condition of entry to a school.

Home–school agreements should be reviewed every two to three years and this can be done through parents' meetings, inviting comments in newsletters or through questionnaires.

of the child is not known, information must be sent within 15 school days of any request from the new school. The duty to forward records does not apply if

- the child has been registered at a school for less than four weeks (although any records from previous schools should be passed on)
- it's not reasonably practical for the headteacher to find out a child's new school
- most recent assessment information is not available (eg. end of key stage assessment results) within 15 days, in which case records can be sent in two parts.

The head must also, upon request, transfer a child's curriculum record to the head of another school where a child is under consideration for admission.

Information for parents

The head must arrange for parents and others to have access to a range of documents, which should be made available on request at all reasonable times. These include

- schemes of work
- syllabuses
- the school prospectus
- circulars
- copies of statutory instruments (where available).

You might also expect the headteacher to arrange for your annual report to be available for inspection at all reasonable times and free of charge at the school. Parents may also ask to see copies of the school policies.

Reporting to parents

At least once during the school year the head is responsible for providing parents of primary school children, from Reception up, with a written report of their child's educational achievements. The report must show, where relevant, the child's results in end of key stage assessments and how these compare with such information about other children at the school and at other schools throughout England (usually described as percentages achieving each level). The report must also state the arrangements under which the report, or issues arising from it, may be discussed with the child's teacher.

Home–school agreements

The governing body is required to have a written home–school agreement in place, drawn up in consultation with parents. The agreement should explain the school's aims and values and the respective responsibilities of the school and of parents, and what the school expects of its children. You must invite parents to sign a declaration in support of the agreement and can also invite children to sign where you consider that the children are sufficiently mature to do so. See 'Outline of a home–school agreement' on the previous page. For more about home–school agreements, see Chapter 5, 'Parents'.

Information to the Secretary of State

The governing body must give the Secretary of State for Education and Skills details of the results of National Curriculum assessments taken. These can then be analysed in preparation for publication. Each year you have to provide information to be used in the primary school performance tables. You have a general duty to make sure that National Curriculum requirements, including the statutory assessment and reporting arrangements, are met. The headteacher must provide the governing body with the results to enable you to comply with national data collection requirements and reporting to parents. Most schools have the administration and marking of tests audited at least once in a four-year cycle. The head and governing body have specific duties to permit the auditor to enter the premises of the school to observe the conduct of tasks and tests and to meet reasonable requests for samples of children's work. Where they have responsibility the headteacher or governing body must submit their national data returns to their LEA as described in the current year's DfES assessment and reporting arrangements (QCA, 2002a, 2002b).

References

DfEE (1995) Circular 10/95. *Protecting Children from Abuse: The Role of the Education Service*. London: DfEE.

DfEE (1999a) *School Admissions Code of Practice.* London: DfEE.

DfEE (1999b) *School Admissions Appeals Code of Practice*. London: DfEE.

DfEE (1999c) Circular 9/99. *Organisation of School Places*. London: DfEE.

DfEE (2000 – revised) Circular 10/99. *Social Inclusion: Pupil Support*. London: DfEE.

DfES (2001a) *Special Educational Needs Code of Practice*. London: DfES.

DfES (2001b) *A Guide to the Law for School Governors – Community Schools (Primary).* London: DfES.

QCA (2002a) *Assessment and Reporting Arrangements for 2002. Key Stage 1*. London: QCA. (Produced annually.)

QCA (2002b) *Assessment and Reporting Arrangements for 2002. Key Stage 2.* London: QCA. (Produced annually.)

Parents

Nigel Gann

Why parents are important to schools

Imagine a school that has the confidence of its parents. By anyone's standards, it's a successful school. Governors and staff have the support and the active participation of the parent body. This makes it possible for them to work most effectively in raising the children's achievement. In this school, parents support their own children's learning. They talk positively about the school in their children's hearing, they show an active interest in what has happened during the day and in their children's work, they encourage their children to do homework and provide the best environment in which to do it. When they are in school, they model pleasant, professional relationships with the school's staff. And they are in school a lot, but always appropriately – working, volunteering, helping, socialising – perhaps even learning themselves. What child could fail to think positively about their school when all this is going on around them?

Can this be your school?

It's the job of the professional staff of the school to provide the children's education. But it's the governing body's job to provide the strategic framework in which this takes place, to hold the headteacher and staff accountable for the standards achieved, and to act as a 'critical friend' to the headteacher throughout these processes (DfEE, 2000b). It's the governing body that determines the ethos of the school, by setting targets and priorities, by agreeing policies and procedures.

It is, therefore, ultimately you who decide

- the ways in which parents can be helped to support their children's learning
- how parents can be encouraged to support the school
- how important parents are, and how they can be valued by the school
- what information should be given to parents, and in what form
- what information should be given about the child, and in what form
- how to share with parents the job of educating the children.

The governing body sets the tone of the school. Because it consists of representatives of all the stakeholders in the school, the governing body is in a position to make a powerful contribution to the relationship between the school and the parents. Consider, for example, the statements that Ofsted asks parents to agree or disagree with in its pre-inspection questionnaire.

- My child likes school.
- My child is making good progress in school.
- Behaviour in the school is good.
- My child gets the right amount of work to do at home.
- The teaching is good.
- I am kept well informed about how my child is getting on.

It's the governing body that determines the ethos of the school

- I would feel comfortable about approaching the school with questions or a problem.
- The school expects my child to work hard and achieve his or her best.
- The school works closely with parents.
- The school is well led and managed.
- The school is helping my child become mature and responsible.
- The school provides an interesting range of activities outside lessons.

(Ofsted, 2000)

Dear Parent,

Thank you to all of you who have continued to support and encourage your children with their weekly homework and spellings. Your involvement is much appreciated. We would be grateful if you would make the daily 15-minute home reading session a priority, whenever possible. There are still a few children who are not yet reading fluently, and at this stage in their learning, it is vital that they receive every possible help and support.

This term at school, your child will be studying the following curriculum topics.

English: Adventure and mystery stories, letter writing, humorous poetry, discussion texts, non-fiction books used for research.

Maths: Number calculations, money and real-life problems, measuring, fractions and decimals, data handling, shapes and angles.

Science: Insulation, solids and liquids.

ICT: Creating patterns using a design package, databases.

Geography: Studying and improving the local environment.

Music: Texture – combining different sounds, orchestral instruments, two-part singing.

PE: Striking and fielding games, athletics, swimming.

RE: Our Church, questions and mysteries.

Art: Textiles.

Design and technology: Sandwich snacks.

Yours sincerely,

Reproduced by kind permission of Norton-sub-Hamdon Church of England Primary School, Somerset.

Each of these is a matter for which the governing body holds ultimate responsibility – and for which it's ultimately accountable to the community served by the school.

So how can you create the framework – and the ethos – in which such positive relationships and attitudes are the norm? How can your school be more like the one described in the introduction? Here we discuss the following suggestions.

- Helping parents to support children's learning and the school.
- Giving useful and interesting information about the school.
- Sharing with parents the job of educating their child.

Creating the framework

Helping parents to support children's learning and the school

Parents will do their best to support their children's learning – after all, parents are their children's first teachers – but they have to know what this means for them. It will be different from school to school, and from family to family. You might set up a consultative group or working party to decide how to develop school-parent relationships. Such a group should include at least some parents and teachers, and might co-opt parents from a variety of backgrounds. This will demonstrate that the school recognises the importance of parents and values them. Here are some of the things that the working party might consider.

1 Regular (eg. half-termly) information about the curriculum to be covered – see the example on the left.

2 Suggestions as to how parents might support learning (conversations, trips, television and videos, books).

3 The purpose and expectations of homework.

4 Introductions to curriculum subjects for parents.

5 'Time to share' – opportunities for parents to see the children's work during or after school.

6 Opportunities for parent helpers in school.

7 The structure of assessment, recording and reporting.

8 Explanations of teaching practices and other processes (for example, strategies for children with special needs, access to music lessons).

Parents will support a school that clearly does its best for their child, and the child will benefit. But the school shouldn't take it for granted that parents will support it without question. It has to earn that support.

Parents expect the school to be professional, open, honest and concerned for their child. But they should also expect it to respect them and their own culture, however different it is. They will recognise that teachers are experts on teaching and learning, as long as teachers and governors recognise that parents are the experts on their own children. Any dialogue between school and parents must be conducted on that premise, whether it is a general debate about school procedures at the annual general meeting, or a discussion of an individual child's progress at a parents' evening.

Parents will support a school that

- recognises their importance and values them
- gives them open, truthful information about the school
- gives honest, frank and useful information about their children
- shares strategies with them, whether they relate to their individual child's learning or to the conduct of the whole school.

Giving useful and interesting information about the school

The governing body is required by law to make certain information available to the parent, through the school prospectus and the annual report to parents. Details of what is needed (which change quite frequently) can be found in the DfEE/NAfW *Guide to the Law for School Governors* and in the relevant updating circulars (DfEE, 2000a; DfES, 2002; NAfW, 2001a). Templates for an annual report to parents and a school prospectus are provided on the accompanying CD-Rom.

But meeting legal requirements should be only the beginning. Any documents issued by the school should be attractively presented, headlined with interesting information, expressed in accessible language and – most importantly – should focus on the work and the activities of the children.

When the school publishes information about children's attainment at the end of Key Stages 1 and 2, you should consider what other achievements are also important. For example, the proportion of children who

- achieve certain reading ages
- participate in extra-curricular activities
- have been abroad with the school
- can eat a meal with a knife and fork
- can throw and catch a ball
- can tie their shoelaces
- play constructively together
- can swim 25 metres
- play a musical instrument
- can use a computer mouse
- have seen a live theatre performance
- can buy items in a shop
- can read a short piece to their class or the school
- engage in circletime.

Statutory requirements

The governing body must provide the following.

- **A prospectus**, which must include
  - details of the school
  - the names of the headteacher and the chair of governors
  - details of the admissions policy
  - the school's ethos and values
  - the school's policy for special educational needs
  - details of religious education
  - any religious affiliations that the school has
  - pupil absence rates
  - National Curriculum test results
  - details of school places and how to apply.
- **An annual report**, which must include
  - details of the annual meeting for parents
  - members of the governing body
  - details about the next parent governor election
  - progress on the action plan following the latest inspection
  - a financial statement
  - information about school security
  - information about access for disabled children
  - information on how the school meets children's special needs
  - a summary of training and professional development undertaken by teachers
  - pupil absence rates
  - National Curriculum test results
  - targets for the next Key Stage 2 results.
- **An annual meeting** for parents to discuss the report and any other matters that parents might raise.
- Details of how to make a **complaint**.

Enhancements

To show that you value the parents and take your accountability seriously, you will also want to make the prospectus attractive and accessible to the whole range of parents and prospective parents – to make it a useful handbook sharing the school's priorities and aspirations (where some of the less interesting, but statutory, information is less prominent). You should also make sure that the annual report

- says and asks as much about the future as it does about the past
- is attractively presented
- contains useful information about what the school is doing and what it intends to do
- is a consultative document that acts as an advert for that event which is potentially (but actually rarely) central to the school's relationships with its parents – the annual meeting.

Notes for governors on responding to parents

Some background

Parents have not always been welcomed into schools, so there are some historical barriers to be broken down. Also, many parents have less-than-pleasant memories of their own schooldays. These circumstances mean that, even in the most welcoming schools (such as ours), there are obstacles to free communication between parents and teachers.

All governors (but especially parent governors) should act as a channel of communication, interpreting the school to its parent community and the parent community to the school.

Some parents – especially those who have got used to other schools – expect schools to blame them when things go wrong. Some schools claim that when parents don't turn up to parents' meetings and other events, it's because they are completely satisfied with the school, or because they are apathetic. It is probable that the answer lies more in the historical obstacles created by schools. Blaming parents is unlikely to help the school to work more closely with them. The following points are worth remembering.

- Parents are the first teachers of their children.
- Children spend less than 15 per cent of their year in school.
- Children's first loyalty is always to their parents.
- It is very difficult for a school to make a difference to a child's life chances without the support of the parents.
- When parents have different expectations of their children from the school's, they are not necessarily wrong!
- Parents' principal relationship with a school is through their own child – their interest in how the school organises itself will always be secondary to that.
- Schools and parents need to work together for the good of the child – schools know a lot about teaching and learning, but parents are the experts on their own children.

If you are approached by parents about an issue in school, remember the following.

- Always refer them first to the headteacher, who is responsible for all organisational matters and for personnel.
- If they are reluctant to speak to the head, offer to accompany them if you can.
- If there is an issue about the headteacher, refer them to the chair of governors (again, offer to accompany them if they are reluctant).
- Always listen sympathetically and carefully to the issue raised, but do not take sides – say that you can only listen at this stage and then investigate. Remember there will always be another side to the story.
- Promise that someone (if not you) will come back to them by a certain date.
- If necessary, point out that they can make a formal written complaint to the governors and/or to the local authority, but that this should be a last resort.
- Whether or not you believe the complaint or problem is not important. Any issue needs to be addressed – the parent is almost certainly expressing their concern in the only way they know how (although the real problem may sometimes be hidden under other concerns).
- When people shout, it's probably because they don't think anyone is listening (and sometimes they're right!). But do not accept aggressive behaviour – always tell the aggressive parent that you will ask the chair or headteacher to contact them.

The annual meeting

Organise an annual meeting that

- takes its place in the school calendar as an opportunity to review (and celebrate) the school's past successes
- asks the parents how they think the school might be even better than it is
- asks parents what they think the priorities might be for the coming year
- asks parents how they think children can best be helped to learn.

The annual meeting is not a token moment in the year when we can blame parents for being apathetic. According to the American political thinker E Schattschneider (1960), 'It is entirely characteristic that responsibility for widespread non-participation is attributed wholly to the ignorance, indifference and shiftlessness of the people.' Nor should we think to ourselves that the reason they don't turn up in huge numbers is that they are so idyllically happy with what the school has to offer. Rather, we must see it as a chance to open up dialogues on all those issues that parents, staff and children think are the most important aspects of the school. If parents are not turning up, it's our fault – because we don't value the opportunities that the annual meeting offers, or because we don't value parents sufficiently. It may even be because we are a bit afraid of what they might say if they did come.

With your fellow governors, think about which events have been well attended recently. Then use your conclusions to influence your decisions about the nature and timing of your annual meeting.

Governing bodies that want parents to come again next year make sure that the way the meeting is organised helps people to express their views – in small groups, for example, or in an informal atmosphere. It gives parents a comfortable environment and an enjoyable – but purposeful – time. It helps you, staff and parents to become a team, helping you to understand each other's perspectives and priorities. If you work on it, your annual meeting can become central to your strategy for parental consultation.

Strategies for good communication

1 Make sure that parents are clear about how to raise issues that concern them throughout the year – by clarifying access to teachers, the headteacher and the governing body, and by making sure that staff and governors know how to deal with (and log) complaints (see 'Notes for governors on responding to parents' on page 87). Some schools decide that teachers will always be available for short meetings without an appointment for half an hour after school on two days a week. Others make it easy for parents to make an appointment. The important thing is that arrangements are appropriate for most of your parents (a school with a lot of commuting parents or working mothers might need different arrangements from a rural school or an inner city one) and

The annual meeting

In the late 1990s, a junior school in an outer London borough was concerned about the small numbers attending the annual meeting. A consultant was called in, and he asked, first, to see their last annual report. He measured the report with a ruler and discovered that just 5 per cent of the report was taken up with things that the governing body had not already decided. The meeting was flagged up to consult with the parents on matters of which 95 per cent had already been agreed (and, in many cases, completed). Who would sit through an annual meeting just to hear a report that they had already received, and on which they could have minimal influence?

In one school, the annual meeting happened on a Thursday in autumn at 10.00 in the morning – because almost all parents, historically, made a habit of attending the Harvest Thanksgiving service (this was an inner-city first school and not a church school). The governors just waited until children had returned to their classes, sat the parents around tables, served coffee and biscuits and asked them to talk about a series of issues.

Other schools have ensured high turnout by combining the meeting with a curriculum information evening or a children's performance. Others offer bribes – wine and cheese or beer and crisps. It depends on the individual school – what works for one won't necessarily work for another.

that the school has made it clear how to get to see a teacher, the head or a governor.

2 Have a well-thought-out media policy (see McClellan and Gann, 2001). Parents will be reassured if they see the school appearing regularly in the local press or TV – for the right reasons! This means appointing someone – a teacher or other staff member, perhaps, or a governor if someone has the right experience – to take responsibility for getting photographs taken, writing short bits of copy and sending them or taking them to the paper.

3 Have a crisis strategy. Occasionally, things go wrong or appear to go wrong. A child gets lost, parents take umbrage against the school for a decision or policy they don't like, staff misbehave – and the news breaks. Sometimes this is mostly a matter of local rumour – we all know how quickly stories get inflated and get around. Sometimes it's more serious than that. Sometimes, tragically, it can involve serious injury or death.

The school should know how it would deal with such events.

- How can all governors be told quickly?
- How can you be sure that only authorised people speak to the media, and that they know how to do that without getting the school in worse trouble?
- How can you be sure that parents who need to be told unpleasant information are told in the most sympathetic way and given appropriate support?
- How can the school show its audience – which will be largely parents and prospective parents – that it's not a victim of circumstances, but that it's able to manage competently and confidently when things don't go according to plan?

Sharing with parents the job of educating the child

Giving useful information about the child

Giving parents information about their children's progress, and dealing with difficulties about the child are among the most important things that schools have to do. How would your school answer these two questions?

1 How important do we think regular consultation with and reporting to parents is in this school?

2 How much in-school training and development time has been devoted to teachers discussing how best to structure these consultations?

See the checklist below.

By law (Education [School Information] Regulations 1998 [as amended by SI 1999/251 and SI 1999/2267]), the school must provide parents with

- access to their children's educational records
- access to schemes of work, syllabuses and statutory documents such as circulars
- an annual written report on their children's educational achievements.

Checklist – talking with parents

The governing body might adopt the following as a code of conduct for meetings between teachers and parents.

- ❑ Always start a formal reporting session by asking the parents in what areas they think the child has made good progress, and where the child has made little or no progress.
- ❑ Show the parents evidence – in written work or otherwise – of any assertions made.
- ❑ Make sure that the conversation is a two-way dialogue.
- ❑ Don't state problems unless you are able to discuss solutions.
- ❑ Don't blame the parents or the child for failing to achieve your expected standards in work or behaviour.
- ❑ Remember that while you may be the expert in teaching, parents are the experts on their own children.
- ❑ If the parents are seeing a number of teachers, make sure that the messages are neither contradictory nor merely repetitive.
- ❑ Consider your own – and the parents' – body language. Look for signs of discomfort and embarrassment.
- ❑ Show you are listening by the way you behave and the way you reflect back the parents' views and feelings.
- ❑ Give plenty of time for the parents to think about and absorb what you are saying. Allow silence to develop new strands of thought.
- ❑ Don't pretend to have answers to everything – even if you think you have!
- ❑ Always finish up the meeting by agreeing strategies. For example, 'What will you do at home, and what will we do at school, to help your child make progress?'.

A good school will recognise that the sharing of information about children's progress is an essential element in diagnosing any problems, in agreeing targets for future achievement, and in motivating children to do better.

So you should make sure that

- the assessment, recording and reporting policy is geared towards making it possible for parents to take part in their children's learning
- meetings between parents and teachers are designed to tell parents what they need and want to know – not just what teachers want to tell them
- the format for these meetings makes it possible for all parents to take part
- staff receive regular training in, or discuss frequently, the communication skills necessary to conduct a parent interview.

The governing body, perhaps working closely with a parents' association, is the best arena for determining the nature of a consultation that involves both teachers and parents. The school might agree on a particular shape or structure to parent meetings – for example, always start with 'Where do you feel your child is making most progress – and least?' and always end with 'And what strategies can we agree now, for school and home, to enable your child to make the best progress?'

A similar consultative process will also come up with the best format for written reports – one which is most informative for parents while not being too demanding for teachers.

Parents don't just want to be presented with problems. Schools and parents must work together to find solutions. As a governor you can help find the best solutions.

Consulting with parents on school strategies

A genuine partnership between school and parents will reflect the range of cultures represented within the community that the school serves. These cultures may be geographical, social, ethnic or religious. But one of your major tasks as a governor is to make sure that the needs and aspirations of the community for its children are being taken into account, and that the interests of all its members are reflected somewhere within the governing body. It's important – especially where the priorities of some parents are very different from those of traditional mainstream schooling – that different, sometimes even opposing, standards are not ignored or condemned.

Legal requirements

Opportunities for sharing information with parents arise in some statutory duties of the governing body.

You must set the framework of a school's behaviour policy through a written statement of general principles that takes account of the needs of all children, including any with special educational needs.

> [Governors] should review this regularly. The statement should cover the ethos of the school, its values and the boundaries of acceptable behaviour; the school's moral code; positive and constructive rules of conduct; and the rewards and punishments to be fairly and consistently applied... The governing body should consult the head teacher and parents of pupils before making or revising the statement, and take account of their views. Consultation could be at their annual meeting for parents or at a specially convened meeting, or in writing.

> The governing body should oversee the headteacher's sound maintenance of discipline at the school in line with their policies. The headteacher has day-to-day responsibility for discipline, with the backing of the governing body. The governing body should advise the headteacher of their views on specific measures for promoting good behaviour. This might include such issues as bullying, racial or sexual harassment, and maintaining regular attendance. The governing body also has a general duty to ensure the school follows policies to promote good behaviour and discipline among pupils.
> (DfEE, 1999; NAfW, 1999)

Since May 2002, schools have also been required to promote race equality and to have a written race equality policy in place.

All this means that you must have a view on what constitutes good behaviour and how to promote it, that you must take the views of the parents into account when developing that view, and that you must monitor behaviour within the school (and inform parents of the results of that monitoring). So you might ask for regular reports from the head on the number of children placed on various disciplinary measures, by age, by gender, by ethnic origin. You might also ask for a breakdown of the times of day when behaviour is most problematic, or the subjects or classes where it is an issue. Where schools have problems with children's behaviour – or where it appears to be deteriorating – governors need more detailed information. Where it's not an issue, you may just ask for routine information on a termly basis. Whatever strategy is agreed, the school should keep parents informed about general trends – if only because the 'we didn't behave like that in our day' syndrome acquires mythical status in every generation.

Schools have to develop – following consultation with parents – a home-school agreement outlining the respective rights and responsibilities of the school, the children and the parents. In the early days, many of these agreements focused on the rights of schools and on the duties of parents. It was entirely typical, for example, for an agreement to specify that parents are required to ensure that their children arrive on time, in uniform, behaving properly with all homework completed. In return, the school might promise to prepare children for the next stage in education, or to help each child achieve his or her potential. While the duties laid on parents are rigorous and easily measurable, it would be a brave parent who set out to prove that the school was failing to meet its promises. The school should commit to absolute measurable undertakings, which it might invite parents to evaluate. One possibility is to set up a governors/PTA panel that could consider annually the school's performance in relation to its home-school agreement and its behaviour policy.

The agreement should be used as another opportunity for the school to strengthen the partnership with parents – to discuss together what behaviour is acceptable and what isn't, to agree what rewards might be useful and what sanctions would be reasonable, and to set out together our expectations of each other. It would, in many cases, be appropriate for governors to lead these discussions.

Other strategies

Although not required by law, many schools are developing interesting practices.

A growing number of schools now use customer survey techniques to establish what their parents and children feel about the service they are getting. Since the University of Keele developed its parent questionnaire in the early 1990s, a number of models have appeared. Some of the best and simplest appeared as a collaboration between the magazine *Managing Schools Today* and the National Union of Teachers. Ofsted has its own questionnaire for the pre-inspection survey. So schools have quite a variety to choose from, and can, of course, develop their own variations. When creating questionnaires

- ask the questions you want answers to
- feed back the results, however uncomfortable that may be
- do something about the issues raised (and tell everyone what you're doing)
- persevere – initial responses may be disappointing, but only because parents are not yet used to being asked, and don't necessarily trust the school's motives
- use a structure and language appropriate to the community you serve – some schools find face-to-face surveys at parents' evenings more useful at first, others create focus groups or take samples rather than trying to address the whole parent body.

See the sample parents' questionnaire on the next page.

Sometimes the information gathered in these surveys can be used to inform an annual whole-school review. At some point in the year (perhaps towards the end of the summer term) all the governors and staff can come together to review the past year – celebrating the successes – and to agree what the school's priorities ought to be for the coming year. Before the meeting you might circulate a questionnaire to parents and children as well as staff and governors. You might also want to invite parents who aren't on the governing body.

Schools and parents must work together to find solutions. As a governor you can help find the best solutions

Parents' questionnaire

Please circle your child's class/year group.

R Y1 Y2 Y3 Y4 Y5 Y6

Please tick the appropriate answer.

My child	Always	Most of the time	Some of the time	Little of the time
Is happy at school.				
Feels safe at school.				
Makes good progress in English.				
Makes good progress in maths.				
Makes good progress in science.				
Makes good progress in information technology.				
Makes good progress in other subjects.				
Makes good progress in social behaviour.				
Is given work at the appropriate level.				
Gets on well with teachers.				
Gets on well with other staff.				
Gets on well with other children.				
Has the right amount of homework.				
Has the right level of homework.				
Feels valued by teachers and other staff.				

As a parent I	Always	Most of the time	Some of the time	Little of the time
Am well informed about my child's progress.				
Am quickly contacted about any problems.				
Understand the school's policies.				
Am consulted about the school's plans and ideas.				
Am asked what I think about the school.				
Am given information about ways I can help with my child's education.				
Feel that the school respects me.				

Parents can also take part in the processes taking place within the school day – in the classroom, in the school office, in the resource centre. Waller and Waller (1998) list the programme of one primary school (see 'Our school's parent participation programme' on page 94).

Being a parent governor

One category of governor has special responsibility for relating to and working with parents. These are the governors elected by the parent body.

The whole governing body shares responsibility for the school's relationships with the children's parents. But if you are a parent governor you have a special duty to reflect the views of parents at governing body meetings. You aren't, though, bound to support those views – you are a representative, not a delegate. The governing body has a statutory duty to keep parents informed about what goes on at governing body meetings by making the agenda, draft minutes, agreed minutes and attached papers available at the school to persons wishing to inspect them (see the Education [School Government] Regulations, 1999 – SI 1999 No.2163, Annex 1 V.40). As a parent governor, you owe it to other parents to fill out those details as far as you can, without breaking confidentiality. That is, you should raise issues but not personalities.

You can do this with the following techniques.

- Take space in any regular newsletter sent to parents with reports from the governing body and its committees, previews of forthcoming topics for discussion and requests for concerns or questions.
- Set up a governors' table at parents' evenings, with information about the governing body and opportunities for queries to be raised.
- Use a section of a noticeboard in a prominent place where parents congregate (a governors' noticeboard near the front of the school, with photographs and pen portraits, is a good idea anyway).
- Wear an identifying badge when you are in school.
- Attend parent teacher association meetings (or ensure that at least one governor does – a PTA link governor is a good idea) – and speak about the governing body's functions.
- Ensure that all parts of the community are reached by consultation processes – perhaps asking for class or year parent representatives.
- Get to know the 'opinion-formers' in various groups of parents – and cultivate them.
- Meet new parents at an early stage (one primary school had all its new parents visited before the child started school – first by a Reception teacher and classroom assistant, then by a pair of governors. The governors would talk about how the parent might relate to the school, how to get information and how to raise concerns.)

Such techniques make it possible for you to speak with greater authority on the governing body. But you also gain a degree of 'democratic legitimacy' that other governors don't necessarily have.

Often, an effective parent governor can warn the governing body and the staff of impending problems. Anyway, you can surely do a great deal to sponsor good relations between governors and parents, and break down some of the misunderstandings that there are among parents about the role and the work of the governing body. This might even help with governor recruitment.

Finally

Conduct your own survey on parent, governor and school relations (for a possible model, see 'Parents and the school – getting it right' on page 95). Remember, these relationships are not a matter of chance. And they are too important to be left only to the teaching staff.

But you should also remember that the school is not a democracy. Nor is it a place where the wishes of every parent – or those of anyone else – can or should be acted upon. Part of your task as a governor is to gather the views of a large number of people – to get a feel of what people want – and then make informed decisions. Sometimes those decisions won't please everyone but you should always have the knowledge and the satisfaction that you are acting in the best possible interests of the children. Often the governing body will be the only group of people to know all the issues and you will usually be the best people to balance short-term concerns with long-term strategy. Respond to parents, consider what they say, make firm decisions and be prepared to justify those decisions at the appropriate times.

Governors have the leading role in getting school–parent relationships right. If you succeed, the beneficiaries are the children. It's their quality of learning, their achievements, their standards which are at stake. The pay-off is huge.

Our School's Parent Participation Programme

Aspect	Elements	Learning support implications
PARENTS INTO SCHOOLS	Parent volunteers in classrooms Parental assistance in running library/school shop Parents and others visiting classes Parent–teacher projects (eg. SMART home reading) Parent–teacher consultations – discussion of progress, review/monitoring of individual education plans Parents offering practical skills (eg. carpentry, maintenance and repairs, reprographics, mounting and displaying work) Parents as governors (foundation and elected parent appointments) Fundraising and support Educational meetings/workshops Induction meetings – pre-school preparation programme	
LINKING WITH HOME	Home visiting by headteacher and other staff – enquiry, fostering relations, imparting information, counselling, discussion of child's progress Telephone and written link Parent representatives (via Parents and Friends Association Committee) Learning/behaviour management programmes (home/school) Home-based learning and curriculum follow-up (eg. SMART) Resource sharing with local community (eg. use of indoor swimming pool on-site/school premises/grounds by outside groups)	
WRITTEN COMMUNICATION	School brochure Information leaflets, books, etc. Illustrated booklets for pupils – preparing for school, secondary transfer Frequent newsletters Eye-catching publicity School noticeboards Assessment, recording and reporting to parents	
FORUMS FOR MEETINGS	Parents and Friends Association (PFA) – fundraising, social, educational and cultural Parent-child induction programme Educational meetings and activity workshops Links with governors – parent governors, governor surgeries, annual parents' meeting Child referral/action/monitoring/review meetings – case discussions involving staff, parents and child – multi-disciplinary gatherings	

Adapted from a framework by Wolfendale (1992b, 2nd ed.) Reproduced by kind permission of the author, Sheila Wolfendale, and the publishers, Cassell plc.

Parents and the school – getting it right

What proportion of parents:

Attend parent–teacher interviews on children's progress?
- Whole school
- By class
- By year
- By child's gender
- By parent's gender
- By geographical community
- By cultural/ethnic community

Attend the annual parents' meeting?
- Whole school
- By class
- By year
- By child's gender
- By geographical community
- By cultural/ethnic community

Attended the last Ofsted parents' meeting?

Ensure that children complete homework most of the time?

Return slips confirming they have read the newsletter?

Return slips confirming they have read an information letter?

Return questionnaires on school performance?

Are staff members at the school?
- Teachers
- Classroom assistants
- Child supervisors
- Catering
- Office administration
- Other

Are volunteer helpers at the school?
- Running clubs or other activities
- Classroom assistants
- Child supervisors
- Office administration
- Other

Are governors?
- LEA
- Co-opted
- Staff
- Foundation
- Other

References

DfEE (1999) *Social Inclusion: Pupil Support, Truancy and School Exclusion* (Circular 10/99). London: DfEE.

DfEE (2000a) *A Guide to the Law for School Governors*. London: DfEE.

DfEE(2000b) *Roles and Responsibilities of Governing Bodies and Headteachers* (0168/2000). London: DfEE.

DfES (2002) *Governors' Annual Reports and School Prospectuses in Primary Schools* (0269/2002). London: DfES.

Gann, N (1998) *Improving School Governance: How better governors make better schools.* London: Falmer Press.

Gann, N (1999) *Targets for Tomorrow's Schools.* London: Falmer Press.

Hallgarten, J (2001) *Parents Exist, OK!? Issues and Visions for Parent-School Relationships*. London: Institute for Public Policy Research.

McClellan, T and Gann, N (2001) *Schools in the Spotlight: A Guide to Media Relations for School Governors and Staff*. London: Routledge Falmer.

National Assembly for Wales (1999) *Pupil Support and Social Inclusion* (NAfW Circular 3/99). Cardiff: NAfW.

National Assembly for Wales (2000) *Roles and Responsibilities of Governing Bodies and Headteachers*. Cardiff: NAfW.

National Assembly for Wales (2001a) *School Governors' Guide to the Law*. Cardiff: NAfW.

National Assembly for Wales (2001b) *Governors' Annual Reports* (NAfW Circular 15/01). Cardiff: NAfW.

Ofsted (2000) *Handbook for Inspecting Primary and Nursery Schools*. London: TSO.

Schattschneider, E (1960) *The Semi-Sovereign People: A Realist's View of Democracy in America*. New York: Holt, Rinehart and Wilson.

Stacey, M (1991) *Parents and Teachers Together*. Milton Keynes: Open University Press.

Waller H and Waller J (1998) *Linking Home and School: Partnership in Practice in Primary Education*. London: David Fulton.

Wolfendale S and Bastiani J (eds.) (2000) *The Contribution of Parents to School Effectiveness*. London: David Fulton.

Staffing

Robin Hammerton

Governors and staff

The staff in your school – teaching and support – are the people who make most things happen. They, you trust, will put your aims and policies into practice and will enable the children to learn well. It's an obvious point, but without the commitment and goodwill of a dedicated, skilled and well-motivated group of staff, your school certainly won't achieve whatever vision you and your headteacher might have.

Basic dos and don'ts

As a governor, you'll want to get to know members of staff, support them in what they're doing and understand their work with the children. You need to know what's happening in the school, and how people are getting on, so that you can make better informed decisions. Some good ways of doing this are outlined in Chapter 2, 'Curriculum'. However, you have to be careful. You shouldn't do anything that might be seen as overstepping the mark (for example, seeking to get involved directly in staff supervision or discussing someone's job description). Managing and leading the staff is the headteacher's job, not yours. Nor is it your job to take up any specific personal issues with the headteacher, or anyone else, on behalf of a member of staff.

Governors' responsibilities for staffing

Notwithstanding the note of warning above, the governing body has several important strategic responsibilities for the staffing of the school. Often these responsibilities are most efficiently carried out outside the main governing body, so you are likely to have a personnel committee, or equivalent. As staffing inevitably uses the bulk of the school's budget, some schools have very successfully established a single committee dealing with both personnel and finance issues, to avoid constant to-ing and fro-ing between two groups.

In broad terms, your responsibilities for staffing, which should be carried out in close partnership with the headteacher, are

- deciding how many people should work in the school, and which kind of staff these should be (remember, your responsibilities cover all employees, not just teachers)
- making suitable arrangements for appointing members of staff and, probably, taking part in these arrangements
- appointing the headteacher
- ensuring the school has a suitable performance management policy, which is carried out
- making sure there are proper procedures in place for staff discipline, capability issues and grievances, and playing a part in the implementation of these policies
- working with the headteacher to make decisions about staff pay in accordance with the school pay policy
- having the power to suspend on full pay, and to dismiss, any member of staff, in appropriate circumstances.

Reading this chapter should help you to know what to do when carrying out each of these responsibilities so that you

- keep the interests of the children and staff at the forefront of your mind
- help the school to move forward
- maintain good relationships
- don't break the law (especially employment legislation)
- take proper account of equal opportunities issues.

Who is the employer?

Different types of school

If yours is a community or voluntary controlled school, then the formal employer of the staff is the local education authority (LEA). The governing body, however, carries out many of the functions of the employer on behalf of the LEA, and it's rare that the LEA can overrule the governing body.

If your school has foundation or voluntary aided status, then the governing body is the formal employer of all staff. This means that you take staffing decisions in your own right and the LEA has even less power to intervene. In these types of school, the governing body – not the LEA – must issue contracts to all staff and you need to have an arrangement in place for this (often carried out by the clerk to the governing body supported by the headteacher).

Different types of staff

Although it's important to know who the formal employer is, this doesn't necessarily affect personnel matters on a day-to-day basis. This particularly applies in the case of teachers, who are all employed in accordance with the School Teachers' Pay and Conditions Act (1991). This gives a very clear legal framework for their work in all schools, whoever the employer is.

There is more flexibility for foundation and voluntary aided schools with the employment of support staff, because any local agreements about terms and conditions don't formally apply. It is therefore possible to negotiate pay and conditions with these staff, specific to your school. However, to opt out of the LEA structures would certainly create a great deal of extra work and difficulty and you would need to be sure the perceived benefits were worth the trouble.

Contracted staff

The governing body has power to enter into contracts, so it's quite possible that some staff in your school work for a contractor you have engaged. Examples might be

- caterers
- grounds maintenance staff
- contract cleaners
- building firms.

While the headteacher will have responsibility for ensuring the contractors carry out their work properly, and may work closely with the staff involved, the governing body has no direct responsibility for the employment of the people involved.

Central LEA staff

There may be teaching and support staff working in your school who are directly employed and managed by the LEA. Examples include

- educational psychologists
- members of support services (for behaviour, for example, or English as an additional language)
- peripatetic music teachers
- staff supporting children with statements of special educational need.

As increasing responsibility is delegated to schools, central staff may be becoming fewer in your school. However, although your headteacher may well manage these staff while in your school, as with contracted personnel, you are not responsible for matters relating to their employment.

Help is at hand

The governing body's responsibilities are considerable and complex. But, remember, the role is strategic and your headteacher will usually deal with personnel matters on a day-to-day basis for you. The head will probably make strategic recommendations about staffing to the governing body or offer options for governors to choose between. In turn, the head should have help from the support package your school buys from the LEA Personnel Service (or an alternative provider, if you prefer). You'll also need to employ a payroll provider (unless you choose to carry out this complicated work yourself, which is almost unheard of in a school).

Recruitment of staff

Schools have freedom

You have to decide how many staff should work at the school, and what type of staff you wish to employ.

This is a very important freedom which, well used, can have a very positive impact on the children's learning and welfare. It's important to understand that there is no set staffing complement from the LEA or anywhere else (though advice may be available). This is down to you as governors – working closely with your headteacher.

The different types of adult you can employ, full or part time, are

- qualified teachers (of different grades and seniority)
- unqualified teachers (instructors) who have special skills and experience that the school

needs and where no suitable qualified teacher is available

- teaching assistants
- administrative and finance staff
- midday supervisors
- ICT technicians
- caretakers (premises/site managers)
- cleaners
- music or sport coaches
- people to lead extra-curricular activities, or those with specialist skills to share with the children.

Perhaps surprisingly, the only person you legally have to employ is a headteacher. After that, it's down to you and your headteacher to make choices within what you can afford. Here are some practical examples of the kinds of issues you can consider.

Teachers and teaching assistants

Teaching assistants (also known as classroom assistants or learning support assistants) can provide excellent support for children's learning. As a matter of policy, you might decide to employ fewer teachers but more assistants. This will lead to larger classes but with extra support. On the other hand, you might consider that, for your school, class size is more important – you would therefore employ more teachers but with less assistant support. If you have infant age-group children in your school, to comply with legislation you'll need to employ enough qualified teachers to ensure that no class goes over 30. You don't have unfettered freedom, but there are choices to make.

Staffing to support the school improvement plan

If, for example, your school planned to strengthen its provision for children with special educational needs (SEN), you might decide to employ a teacher as an SEN coordinator who is not class based, or to fund significant release time from class. Perhaps it would be more useful to employ a teaching assistant specifically for SEN than one who is to be attached generally to a class. Or you could choose to buy in extra time from an LEA support service that will meet the children's needs.

As a school, you might have a specific school improvement plan target to improve achievement in literacy, ICT or sport, for example. If so, you might want to employ someone with specialist skills in the chosen area, balancing this against what might not receive such attention elsewhere.

Management and leadership

It's up to the school to decide how its management structure will be organised. Most schools have at least one deputy headteacher, but this is not compulsory. It's also possible to employ other senior teachers.

- Assistant headteachers, responsible for particular aspects of school life.
- Advanced skills teachers, who have excellent classroom skills to share with others.
- Fast-track teachers, who are destined for headship and who can work in your school for about two years on the way, seeking to develop rapidly an aspect of your provision and to learn management skills. Schools have to apply to the Fast Track Central Support Team, part of the DfES, to be allowed to employ a fast-track teacher.
- Teaching staff being paid management allowances for specific responsibilities (say, the leadership of a key stage or a major area such as assessment, numeracy or literacy).

From time to time, with the headteacher, you should consider what management and leadership structure suits the school best.

The school office

The school will certainly need good administrative and finance support. From time to time, you should consider whether the provision is adequate and effective for current needs.

Combining roles

It's also possible to integrate jobs, so that the same person could be carrying out more than one support staff role. This can sometimes make recruitment easier (as the job is bigger), as well as encouraging greater consistency and understanding across different areas of school life.

All of these different possibilities can help create exciting opportunities for children.

Think before you replace

If your budget allows, your school may be able to create new posts. Often, however, the chance to recruit occurs when someone leaves. It can be sad when a valued member of staff moves on and you may wonder how you will ever replace them. However, your first thought should not necessarily be to replace like with like. Perhaps this is an opportunity to bring in someone with different skills and ideas that your school now needs. Maybe it provides a chance for the headteacher to reorganise things and for some existing staff to move into new roles in the school. Think afresh.

Staff development

Staff development isn't something that applies only to teachers. Providing opportunities for the development of all staff is a way for the school to show that it values people. It is also – very importantly – a way of making sure and demonstrating that the school wants staff who are best equipped to provide the best possible educational provision for children.

Certainly staff development is likely often to involve people attending courses – either in or out of school time. It can also involve such things as staff discussions, reading, observation, on-line training and reflective journals.

Your school will almost certainly have a professional development coordinator whose role is to make sure that the right opportunities are made available and that the appropriate part of the budget is well spent. Your role as a governor is not to get involved in the detail of the professional development activities but to assure yourself that these activities benefit the school as a whole as well as the individual members of staff. To do this you will expect to receive regular reports – probably within the termly report of the headteacher – about what has been happening, what is planned and how it all fits in with the school development and improvement plans.

Staff development and recruitment

This brings us to another important point. It's sensible to think of employing new staff alongside the development of your existing personnel. Training and support may make it possible for a current member of staff to take on new responsibilities, thus changing your recruitment needs. As a governor, you're unlikely to be involved directly in staff development and training but it's helpful to use information from the headteacher about this area when you're involved in making recruitment decisions.

The recruitment process

Make a policy

The governing body is responsible for appointing all staff in the school. However, this certainly doesn't mean that you should be doing all of the work. Much of the responsibility may be delegated to the headteacher and there can also be an important role for other senior staff who might not be governors. There is no place in a well-run school for any turf wars or misunderstandings in this area, so you need a clear school policy, or appointments procedure, to say what happens and who does what at each stage of the process.

Key principles

The key principles that your school staff appointment procedures should follow, and which should be mentioned in the policy, include

- the intention to recruit a high-quality staff, well suited to the school's needs
- a clear partnership between the headteacher, governors and appropriate school staff in making appointment decisions
- openness, fairness and equal opportunities for all candidates.

You'll also need to be careful that your appointments procedure doesn't become cumbersome and bureaucratic, with committees having to meet to ratify every minor detail. It's wise to leave the management of the process to the headteacher, perhaps working in consultation with the chair of the personnel committee. It can be hard to recruit good staff and often the number of applicants may be small. Schools that can't get their act together swiftly, and then be responsive to what they find happening in the market place, will be doubly disadvantaged.

Stages of appointment

Once you've identified a vacancy, the school will need to put together a timetable and make arrangements for

- advertising the post
- sending out information to potential candidates
- informal visits to the school
- receiving applications, shortlisting and taking up references
- interviewing and appointment.

You must give people enough time to see the advertisement, respond to it and then apply (two weeks is a respectable minimum), but try not to let the process drag on.

1 Advertising the post

Every job vacancy in your school should be advertised. This satisfies principles of fairness and equal opportunities. Advertisements, as appropriate, may be placed

- internally, for current staff only (incidentally, if a promoted post is being advertised externally, it will be important to make it clear that current staff are invited to apply on the same basis as those from outside)
- in a school newsletter
- locally (say, in the press and LEA bulletin)
- nationally.

The purpose of the advertisement is to attract as many suitable applicants as possible. Therefore, it needs to say briefly

- why the school is a good place to work and what opportunities will be available in this job

Model specification for a senior teaching post

Essential experience/qualities	Desirable experience/qualities
Qualified teacher status	A degree or evidence of higher-level study
At least *x* years' successful teaching experience in the age range specified	Experience of working with all age groups in the school
Evidence of effective leadership in a school – for example in a curriculum subject	Able to offer evidence of successful involvement in the management of change or in a specific initiative
Able to give evidence of good teamwork skills and ability to form cooperative, friendly relationships with children, colleagues and parents	Experience of leading cooperative curriculum planning, INSET or policy development
Able to show a thoughtful approach to issues concerning teaching and learning, assessment and school improvement	Successful experience of monitoring and supporting the work of others
Clear willingness to follow whole-school decisions and policies, to lead other staff in doing so, and ability to contribute constructively to the policy-making process	Understanding of the role of mentor (of a newly qualified teacher, for example); willingness to develop in this role
Good understanding of, and experience with, current national initiatives	Experience or understanding of coordinating school events
Committed to further professional development	Good sense of humour

Notes: Church schools, or other schools with a religious character, can include religious criteria in their specifications.

Your school could use and adapt this model to suit your needs and the particular requirements of the post.

Interview questions would need to relate to the statements in the specification.

Model specification for a teaching assistant

Essential experience/qualities	Desirable experience/qualities
Evidence of a positive, mature, caring personality, particularly in relation to children	Experience of a similar kind of work, paid or unpaid
Willing and able to contribute to children's learning and welfare	Qualifications in child care or an appropriate subject
Able to communicate clearly in writing and verbally	Experience or understanding of children with special needs
Able to work within a team environment and under supervision	A self-starter with good initiative
Able to follow specific instructions closely	Interests that could be shared with groups of children
Able to form good relationships with colleagues and parents	Willing to take part in individual and whole-staff training positively
Able to be discreet when needed and to maintain confidentiality	
Happy to help out wherever reasonably needed	

Notes: Your school could use and adapt this model to suit your needs and the particular job description of the post.

Interview questions would need to relate to the statements in the specification.

- basic details of the responsibilities of the post
- whether the position is full time or part time, permanent or fixed term
- when the post will begin
- the scale/salary being offered
- how the person can respond to the advertisement and who they should contact at the school.

It needs to say enough to whet the appetite, but without too much detail.

2 Sending out information to potential candidates

More detail will be necessary for the pack of information to be sent to people who respond to the advertisement. This pack should be attractive and include

- a friendly letter, probably from the headteacher, including details of the post and appointment procedures
- a job description for the post
- a person specification, which outlines the criteria that will be used to select the new member of staff
- an application form.

The purpose of this pack is, again, to encourage suitable people to apply. So its tone needs to be positive as well as accurate and realistic.

See the 'Model specifications' on page 101.

3 Informal visits to the school

Prospective candidates may wish to visit the school before applying. The headteacher will normally be the one who organises this. For people living farther away, or who cannot visit, it's good for the headteacher to be able to answer any questions by telephone.

4 Receiving applications, shortlisting and taking up references

If, on deadline day, the school has received a good field of applicants, then a shortlisting process will be needed and chosen candidates will need to be invited to interview. It's helpful to ring them first and follow up the phone call with a letter. Unsuccessful candidates should also be contacted sympathetically. The headteacher may undertake the shortlisting alone, or with someone else, according to your policy. If a group of people does the shortlisting, ideally this should be the same as the interview panel. It is important that shortlisting is done only in accordance with evidence that the application forms give about how well the candidates match up to the person specification.

Confidential references should be taken up for the shortlisted candidates and these should be made available to the interview panel.

If you don't have enough candidates to make a shortlist, you may wish to re-advertise the post. Alternatively, you may have just one candidate who appears strong. If so, subject to your headteacher's advice, consider going ahead with the interview anyway. You only need one good candidate to appoint. However, if neither of these options appears suitable, then you should re-evaluate the situation – is there any other way you could fill this gap in the short or long term from within existing resources? Could you try advertising another type of post? Another possibility would be to use the services of a supply or recruitment agency.

5 Interviewing and appointment

Your policy should

- identify who should be on the interview panel for each type of post
- vest the power to make the appointment, on behalf of the governing body, in the interview panel or the headteacher.

It may well be that the involvement of governors is different for different types of staff. For example, the appointment of main grade teaching staff, teaching assistants and other support staff could be delegated completely to the headteacher working with senior staff. Higher-ranking posts might have more governor involvement. This is for you to discuss and decide with the headteacher. The question to consider is – what might each representative role bring to the process which will add value? It may seem harsh, but if the answer seems to be 'little', don't include that role. In any case, a sensible number for most interview panels would be two to five people.

> Regulations resulting from the Education Act 2002 are likely to decrease the extent to which governors have to be directly involved in identifying vacancies and in filling them. Yours will be the responsibility to determine an overall staffing framework and a budget. The headteacher will then decide on all appointments outside the leadership group. The headteacher will also decide on any staff dismissals, with a committee of the governing body acting as an appeals panel.

Useful interview questions for teaching and support posts

What led you to apply for this job?

Tell us about your experience of...

What particular qualities do you have to bring to this job?

What kind of teams have you worked on? What part did you play?

Tell us about when you've worked under supervision. How was this?

In this school, we are working hard to develop ... What could you bring to help this?

Describe an achievement in your current job/training course/life outside work that you're very proud of.

Tell us about a successful initiative you have been involved with or led.

How would you deal with a parent who was obviously concerned about an incident in school that day?

Do you have any interests that you could share with the children?

Interview questions likely to be useful for teaching posts

What is your classroom like? (Or – What would you want your classroom to be like?) Why?

What, in your view, are the most important features of a good primary education? Why?

Tell us about a really good lesson/series of lessons you've taught. Why were you so pleased with it/them?

How have you helped a colleague to reflect on or improve their professional work?

How do you organise assessment in your classroom? What part do children play in assessing their learning?

What are your teaching strengths? What areas would you like to develop further?

Before the interview, the panel should establish, with the headteacher's guidance, a set of questions, which will be same for each of the candidates, based on the person specification. Each panel member needs to know which questions they will be asking. This doesn't preclude asking follow-up questions, or seeking clarification based on individual candidates' replies. But it does ensure that you are fair to everyone.

The panel must avoid asking personal questions about the candidates' marital status, trade union membership, home circumstances or childcare arrangements.

In a good interview situation

- candidates should be offered a comfortable area to wait beforehand, with suitable toilet facilities and access to tea and coffee
- things should run broadly to time
- the chair of the interview panel should introduce all panel members to each interviewee, and try to ensure that candidates are made to feel at ease, so they can give of their best and answer fully
- note-taking by panel members should be as unobtrusive as possible
- at the end of the questioning by the panel, each candidate should have the opportunity to add anything else they wish that hasn't been mentioned so far and to ask any questions of the panel
- candidates should be informed how they will be told the outcome of the interview.

It's possible to include in the interview process features such as candidate presentations and 'in tray' exercises. This is likely to be most relevant to senior posts and more is said about it in the next section.

At the end of the interview process, hopefully the panel will come to a decision and the right appointment will be made. Congratulations! The headteacher may give a debriefing to unsuccessful candidates. The job offer to the successful candidate will usually be given orally to begin with.

The Criminal Records Bureau (CRB) provides a 'one-stop-shop' service with access to criminal records information held on the police national computer, the DfES 'List 99' which identifies people whose employment in the education service has been barred or restricted and the Department of Health's Protection of Children Act List. Your LEA is registered with the CRB and will go about getting the appropriate disclosure for anyone offered a post at the school.

Volunteers working at the school are also subject to checks. As a governor you are regarded as a volunteer and the LEA will be expected to apply for disclosure when you are re-elected or reappointed.

Information about the CRB and about other pre-appointment checks is provided in a Guidance document from the DfES. (DfES, 2002)

Let's be very clear at this point about one thing – appointing a headteacher is for the governing body alone

Assuming this is accepted, it should be followed up in writing, and made subject to

- satisfactory criminal record and medical checks
- verification that qualifications – especially teaching qualifications – claimed by the candidate are actually held (you could ask candidates to bring teaching certificates to the interview)
- for teachers, that they are, or can be, registered with the General Teaching Council (GTC).

For more about interviews, see the box 'Useful interview questions' on page 103.

Appointing headteachers and deputy headteachers

Of all the duties governing bodies have, appointing the headteacher is perhaps the most important. It's a serious responsibility but also a great opportunity. This section offers practical help for undertaking this task, as well as giving some complementary guidance for selecting a deputy headteacher.

It's your call

At this point, let's be very clear about one thing – appointing a headteacher is for the governing body alone. Legally, the LEA chief education officer, or their representative, has the right (but not a duty) to be present at all meetings of the governing body concerning the appointment of a headteacher, including the interviews. You, as governors, are obliged to consider any advice offered. In all probability, LEA support throughout the process will be very helpful to you, and welcome. However, the fact remains that the LEA contribution to the headteacher selection procedure, however authoritative, is still only advice. All the decisions about the process and final appointment, without exception, are yours as governors.

Some key points

A new headteacher means change

When a new headteacher arrives in school there will be change. This doesn't mean there will be a revolution or that all that has gone before will suddenly disappear. However, if nothing else, there will almost certainly be immediately noticeable differences in style.

If the school has been experiencing some problems, then a new approach may be much wanted. On the other hand, if your school is broadly successful, and the previous headteacher has done a good job over a period of time, then the prospect of change, however moderate and carefully planned, may not be so welcome. But change will come anyway. As a governing body, you need to understand this and embrace the opportunity it brings. You may need to share these thoughts, sensitively, with the staff. However good your school is, and however much the previous head will be missed, appointing a new head gives the prospect of fresh impetus and positive development.

Give out the right messages about your school

When you're sending out information to prospective candidates, it's natural to want to tell them just how good the school is, that the standards are high, the staff is highly committed,

and so on. Even if all this is true, be careful how you present it. Of course you want to give a good impression. It's absolutely right to be loyal to the outgoing headteacher. But, to have the best chance of attracting really strong candidates, it's also helpful to give the clear signal that the new appointee is going to have scope to move the school forward. If the message you give, however inadvertently, is that the school is doing just fine, and you're looking for someone to keep things ticking along, then you may not attract the best candidates.

You should draw applicants' attention to any specialisms or initiatives the school is pursuing. If your school has some difficulties, say what you've done so far to address them. This will tell candidates that the school knows where it's going. At the same time, try not to overplay this, as you could put off good people with other areas of expertise to offer.

Don't lose your head!

Your outgoing head should play no direct part in selecting the successor. However, there are some useful things that they can do. For example

- helping to produce the materials going out to candidates (the current head is likely to know what will motivate people to apply)
- supporting and helping governors through the process
- arranging for the practicalities of placing the advertisement and sending out details to candidates
- being available to show prospective candidates around the school and discussing the post informally
- being around during the interviews to support the candidates and smooth the process along.

How many hoops to jump through?

When you interview candidates for the post of headteacher, you'll want to test them against your person specification. There are many different techniques you can use, including

- formal interviews
- candidate presentations to a panel
- informal buffet with staff and governors
- in-tray exercises, in which candidates are asked to say how they would deal with possible scenarios
- written tasks, for example, a letter to a hypothetical parent
- observed discussions between candidates and children
- observed group tasks undertaken by the candidates themselves
- candidates teaching lessons watched by panel members.

It can be tempting to include as many of these as possible and to be seen to be thorough. But it's helpful to bear in mind that putting candidates through several hoops doesn't increase the quality of those candidates. It could, on the other hand, tire them (and you) out, or even put them off coming to your selection process at all. It's wise to choose a smaller number of activities that will provide the information you need and give the candidates the opportunity to perform at their best.

The formal process

When appointing a head or deputy, you'll be following broadly the same procedure for all staff outlined earlier in the section 'Stages of appointment', starting with advertising the post and, hopefully, concluding with making a successful appointment. The following conditions also apply.

- Posts must be advertised nationally (the *Times Educational Supplement* is the most usual place).
- The governing body must inform the LEA formally of the vacancy and, in the case of headship, of who is on the shortlist for interview.
- Successful candidates must have full qualified teacher status.
- There must be at least three governors on the selection panel.
- The recommendation of the selection panel of the candidate for appointment must be put before the full governing body for ratification.
- A candidate holding the National Professional Qualification for Headship (NPQH) is judged to have met the demanding national standards for headteachers. First-time headteachers appointed from 1 April 2004 are likely to need to hold, or be working towards, the NPQH.
- For deputy headteacher appointments, the LEA has the same rights to be present as it does for headship. The LEA is less likely to take up these rights, unless paid, as the headteacher will be your chief advisor and professional leader, and also the person with whom the new deputy is likely to work most closely in future.

If no appointment is made, posts can, of course, be re-advertised.

Performance management is the appraisal process by which, under law, all teachers have their work assessed

Acting appointments and secondments

To fill any short-term gaps, you are able to appoint suitable people to act as deputy head or head. The LEA may be able to help you find someone if there is no one suitable within the existing staff, perhaps by brokering a secondment from another school.

In the same way, it's possible that your governing body may be asked by the LEA to consider seconding one of your senior staff elsewhere for a period. When considering any such request, it's important to bear in mind

- the possible effects on your own school
- the benefits that may accrue to another school or the LEA
- the wishes and needs of the member of staff concerned.

Performance management and pay

Performance management is the appraisal process by which, under law, all teachers have their work assessed. Performance management outcomes may influence pay decisions for senior teaching staff, including the headteacher. All schools need to have working polices for performance management and pay.

This section outlines the main issues involved and what governors need to do about them, as well as what must be left to the headteacher and staff.

Performance management

The governing body has three duties relating to performance management. These are

1. to establish the school's performance management policy
2. to ensure the performance management policy is working well
3. to review the performance of the headteacher.

The headteacher has the responsibility for implementing the policy.

How you might view performance management

As a compulsory national scheme that may be linked to pay, performance management may create wariness among staff. In some schools, therefore, something that can and should be a constructive process may be reduced in its effectiveness. When the headteacher reports to governors on performance management in the school, it's more helpful for you to focus on how the school has achieved the spirit and intention, rather than the letter, of the regulations. This won't involve disobeying the law, but rather encouraging a process that is

- supportive, as well as honest and rigorous
- based on trust
- understood as a way of improving teaching and learning
- user-friendly and non-bureaucratic for all concerned
- used to identify the right development areas and opportunities for staff.

Model performance management form for all staff

(Boxes can be expanded to make this form, which straightforwardly covers the whole process, no more than two sides of A4.)

Name of staff member: ______________________________

Objectives for the year	Progress during the year
To save time afterwards, fill in this column during the meeting. These objectives need to be very clear. They should take account of the SDP, target-setting and the staff member's own needs.	Please fill in this section as the year progresses.

Development and training needed to support objectives

Development and training that would be useful	Progress during the year
Please fill in this column during the objectives meeting.	Please fill in this section as the year progresses.

Objectives and training needs agreed by: ______________________________

Post holder: ______________________________ Team leader: ______________________________

Date: ______________________________

Review statement: Performance assessment, completed by team leader

Please fill in this section during or soon after the review meeting. This should help to set objectives for the following year.

Statement agreed by: ______________________________

Post holder: ______________________________ Team leader: ______________________________

Date: ______________________________

Performance management policy

You need a performance management policy for your school. Although there is a useful national model, your policy needs to be specific to your situation. It should contain the following components.

1 A brief statement about philosophy

This could state that, although much of the policy is nationally prescribed, the school is committed to using the performance management system to develop all staff, improve teaching and raise standards of achievement for all children.

2 Details of who the policy applies to

Legally, the policy need only apply to teaching staff, but the school may choose to include all support staff. Newly qualified teachers take part in an induction process, with a senior member of staff as mentor. They join the performance management system when this is completed successfully, usually after one year.

3 Organisational arrangements

The basic process is that each staff member discusses and agrees individual objectives with a team leader, appointed by the headteacher, and these objectives are recorded. The team leader reviews the individual's ongoing progress and, after a year, writes a formal statement.
The process then begins again. Additionally, there needs to be a complaints procedure.

4 Principles of confidentiality

The appraisee and the headteacher are the only people who hold copies of the individual objectives and statements. Governors may only see individual statements if they are involved in taking decisions about that teacher's pay.

5 How performance management links to the school development or improvement plan

It's important that staff objectives should relate to the needs of the school as well as to those of the individual.

Performance management for the headteacher

The performance management process for the headteacher is broadly the same as for other members of staff. Differences are that

- the team leader role is taken by a committee of governors
- the process is supported by an external professional advisor
- the chair of governors and head hold the only copies of the formal statement, which is, of course, confidential.

If you sit on this committee, remember that if the process is to be effective for the children, it's important that both you and the headteacher come out of the dialogue with positive feelings. With your headteacher, try to establish trust – and your shared ground rules – before meeting the advisor.

See the 'Model performance management form for all staff' on page 107.

Common staffing policies and procedures: a checklist

- ❑ **Induction policy** for new staff and those changing roles in the school
- ❑ **Staff capability procedure**
- ❑ **Staff conduct procedure**
- ❑ **Staff grievance procedure**
- ❑ **Appointments procedure** for teaching and support staff
- ❑ **Staff absence policy**
- ❑ **Equal opportunities policy** (good practice in equal opportunities issues should ideally pervade all your policies and practices)
- ❑ **Pay policy**
- ❑ **Performance management policy**
- ❑ **Staff development policy** outlining the school's commitment to the development of all staff and the ways it achieves this – how decisions are made about courses and other training and development opportunities

Pay

The governing body (with the support of the headteacher) is responsible for producing a pay policy, which explains

- the school's intention to be a good employer
- how equal opportunities are assured for all staff
- how staff are initially placed on appropriate salary scales
- the management structure of the school and allowances paid for particular responsibilities
- how staff pay reviews are carried out
- that pay matters are kept confidential except where there is a genuine 'need to know'
- how teachers and support staff may, exceptionally, be denied incremental pay points on their basic pay spines, due to unsatisfactory performance
- the criteria under which teachers who have passed threshold assessment may progress further on the upper pay spine
- where decision-making is delegated to any staffing or personnel committee
- that the policy was written in consultation with the staff.

Decisions you may need to take about pay

Bear in mind that teachers' pay structures are governed by the legally binding *School Teachers' Pay and Conditions Document*, published annually by the DfES. You must work within the provisions of this document, and there are various issues that you may need to consider.

1 Members of the leadership group

'Leadership group' means the headteacher and any deputy and assistant heads. The governing body has to set a salary range for each staff member on the leadership spine, based on the group size of the school. Each year, you must review the salaries of the leadership group, taking account of the performance management review of each person and, for deputy and assistant heads, the advice of the headteacher.

2 Teachers on the basic pay spine

The progress of teachers along the basic pay spine is virtually automatic, with annual increments. Even so, these awards need to be formally ratified by governors on the headteacher's advice.

3 Teachers on the upper pay spine

Teachers who reach the top of the basic pay spine may apply to the headteacher to cross the threshold, involving assessment of their work against several criteria, ratified by an external assessor. If successful, the teacher moves to the upper pay spine and the pay differential comes directly into the school's budget. You play no role in this process. However, once on the upper pay spine, teachers may progress up a further four pay points on the recommendation of the headteacher and approval by governors according to the pay policy. This involves headteacher and governors considering the teacher's performance management review and, probably, affordability. Although some government funding is available, there is no guaranteed payment to the school to finance progression up the upper pay spine.

4 Teachers with additional allowances

In accordance with the school pay policy and advice from the headteacher, governors can award set allowances to teaching staff not in the leadership group for

- management responsibilities
- recruitment and retention
- working with children with special needs.

You can award these permanently or on a time-limited basis (for the duration of a special task that a teacher is leading, for example).

5 Support staff

Progress of support staff along local authority pay scales is usually automatic, and may not need any governing body action. However, governors, with the headteacher, carry out the initial placement of support staff on the appropriate scale, and any promotion to a new scale.

Conditions of service and formal procedures

For an overview, see the checklist of 'Common staffing policies and procedures' on page 108.

Working hours

Support staff

Technically, the hours of all support staff are counted. This means that staff are contracted to work a certain number of hours per week, possibly in term time only. These hours are determined by the relevant committee, working with and through the headteacher, in consultation with the staff member. The committee should agree any subsequent changes on the headteacher's recommendation.

Teaching staff

For teaching staff, hours worked are governed by the Teachers Pay and Conditions Act. The question of workload is an area of controversy for the unions. This is because, although teachers can be directed by the headteacher to attend during school hours and events like staff meetings, hours for work such as marking and lesson preparation are, in theory, unlimited.

In your school, these matters are for the headteacher to manage with the teaching staff. Much depends on goodwill. You can certainly ask the headteacher how things are organised but you must not become directly involved.

Job descriptions

Although you appoint teaching and support staff to particular responsibilities, the provision and agreement of job descriptions are for the headteacher.

Leave of absence

Staff absence is almost inevitably disruptive to children's learning. At the same time, you'll want to be a good, fair employer. This is an area where your school can avoid any unnecessary misunderstandings or discontent by having a clear policy, available to all staff. You can obtain advice about what to include from your local education authority and you will almost certainly want to adopt the LEA's model policy, which will have been drawn up with legal advice and in consultation with the relevant unions.

Broadly speaking, types of leave to which staff members are entitled are

- paid sickness absence
- annual (holiday) leave, taken mainly in the school holidays
- maternity and paternity leave

Practical tips for dealing with staff issues

DO

- Get to know the staff and the issues they deal with day by day.
- Share in and celebrate the successes of the headteacher and staff.
- Discuss things with, and support, your headteacher.
- Remember that you, the governing body, are not there to manage the staff.
- Include support staff as well as teachers in your thinking.
- Draw on your experience to encourage staff who may be working under pressure (a friendly word or small piece of practical help, at the right time, can do wonders).
- Respect confidential information about staff.

DON'T

- Take up too much of the staff's time – they should welcome your interest, but are also very busy!
- Do anything that could undermine the headteacher with the staff or parents.
- Agree to take up individual grievances or issues on behalf of any member of staff.
- Give any impression of trying to tell the staff how to do their jobs, however unintentionally.

- statutory unpaid parental leave
- reasonable unpaid absence to deal with a family emergency involving a dependant which could not be foreseen, or alternative arrangements made.

Types of leave the school may give at its discretion include

- special (or compassionate) leave, paid or unpaid
- time away for religious observance
- leave for public service (say, as a magistrate – or school governor!)
- study leave.

Your policy should state the circumstances under which all types of leave can be applied for and granted. It is usually sensible for the governing body to delegate decisions to the headteacher, as other arrangements can become unwieldy. You can protect the headteacher by allowing them to consult the governing body in individual cases, if necessary.

Finally, you need to make sure your school has insurance, or arrangements through the LEA, to cover the potentially high costs of staff absence unless the governing body decides it's best to take the risk and self-insure as a matter of policy.

Industrial action

From time to time, staff may join in with industrial action, which could include striking. You may or may not have sympathy with the cause. Whatever, the headteacher will have to make arrangements to deal with the consequences, which could include children having to stay at home. As a governing body, you are well advised not to seek to influence the headteacher's decision about this because the headteacher is in the best position to decide what is most appropriate, especially about children's well-being and safety. Also, you need to keep good working relationships afterwards.

Redundancy and redeployment

Perhaps as a result of falling rolls or budgets, it may become necessary to make someone redundant. Naturally, you'll do your best to avoid this and hope, perhaps, that natural wastage will resolve the problem. Failing this, a voluntary redundancy would be preferable to a compulsory one. Your LEA might be able to organise redeployment to another school, or post, for your member of staff.

If a redundancy is being considered, you'll want to maintain morale and goodwill. Remember that, in law, a redundancy is a dismissal, so you have to get it right.

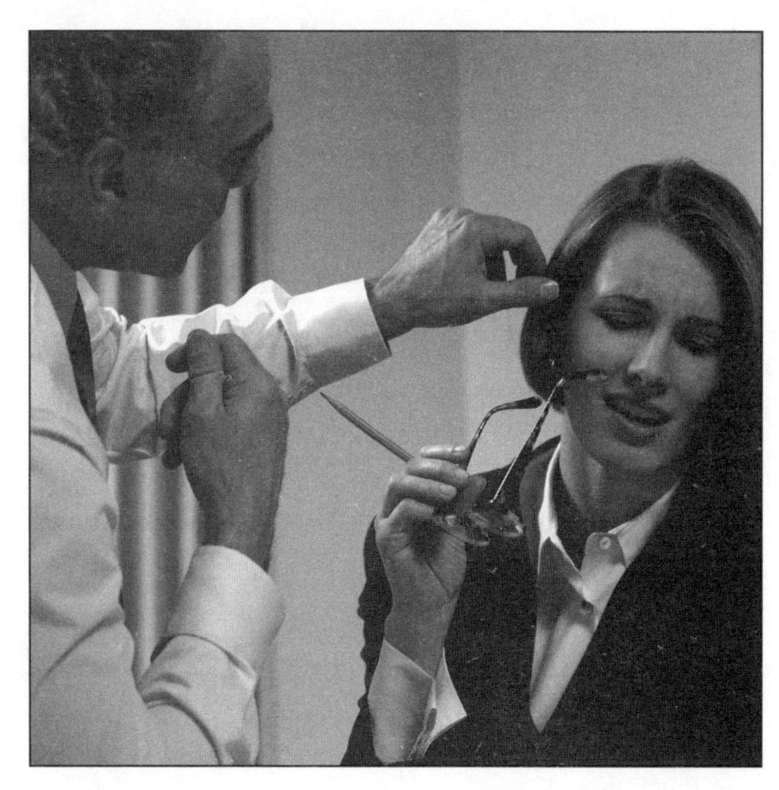

Therefore, it's important to

- be open and up-front with the staff, typically through the headteacher
- be sensitive to staff feelings
- ensure that the school has a proper, fair redundancy procedure in place, which makes the criteria for selecting the person clear and involves consultation with trade unions, as appropriate
- work closely with the LEA and follow their advice (the costs of not doing so could be very high – and higher still if you're considering early retirement as an option).

Staff conduct and capability

Conduct

Your school needs to have a policy for staff conduct and discipline, though, with luck, it will never be needed. Again, you can obtain advice about what to include from your local education authority and you will almost certainly want to adopt the LEA's model policy, which will have been drawn up with legal advice and in consultation with the relevant unions.

Your school needs to have a policy for staff conduct and discipline, though, with luck, it will never be needed

This will provide for a series of warnings to be given by the headteacher to any member of staff whose conduct is causing concern, and for an investigation to happen. (If the headteacher's conduct is in question, the chair of the governing body must take the action.) Normally, this is all on a need-to-know basis. Some governors must be uninvolved as they may have to hear the case later. Therefore, if matters are resolved, you may never know the procedure was ever started.

However, if the misconduct persists, the head may bring the case and all the evidence to the governing body's staff dismissal committee. Should the misconduct be gross (an assault or the theft of school property, say) then one single incident can be enough to recommend dismissal.

Suspension from duty

The headteacher or the governing body may suspend any member of staff on full pay if it seems necessary. This is a very serious step to take with possible repercussions for morale, but in itself it should not be seen as condemning the person. A misconduct procedure doesn't necessarily require a suspension. It would be difficult for governors to suspend a member of staff, other than the headteacher, without the headteacher either having already made the suspension or at least being in agreement. Only the governing body may reinstate after suspension.

Capability

Children are entitled to be taught by competent staff, who are concerned for their own professional development and that of the school as a whole. By law, governing bodies must have procedures for dealing with lack of capability. There is a DfES model for teaching staff (DfES, 2000).

Capability issues are very different from those relating to conduct. Here, the member of staff is not behaving badly but struggling with their work. The procedure is concerned, therefore, with offering opportunities for the person to improve by setting them time-limited targets and supporting and monitoring their progress.

The headteacher will formally instigate and manage this process, which can last up to about 24 weeks. However, where the children's education is in jeopardy, there can be a short procedure of up to four weeks. Whichever applies, hopefully the work of the person improves and the procedure ends, in which case governors may never know about it. If, however, things don't progress and improve, the headteacher may bring the case to the staff dismissal committee.

Staff dismissal committee

This committee, of at least three governors, is to hear cases under both the conduct and capability procedures. If you are a member, bear in mind the following points.

- Children deserve good staff who behave properly and who are competent. Dismissal may well be the only proper option.
- Your decision could be challenged at an employment tribunal. LEA or other professional advice to you and the headteacher is, therefore, essential.

A member of staff who is dismissed may appeal to a new panel of governors who were not involved the first time round.

Grievance procedure

The governing body should have a grievance procedure to try to resolve cases where staff feel they have been treated unfairly or maliciously and where informal methods have not worked.

Generally, the headteacher should hear any grievances, perhaps with a senior colleague or representative governor, unless they relate to the head, when a panel of governors will step in.

If you're ever involved in this, remember that the ideal outcome is one where each party is satisfied, with honour and respect being maintained. You therefore need to be completely fair. This doesn't mean that you shouldn't form a view about the rights and wrongs, but you should try to find common ground where possible. Your aim, if possible, is to reach a point where all involved understand each other and can move forward.

Finally

Some down-to-earth pointers for governors dealing with staffing issues are given in the 'Practical tips for dealing with staff issues' on page 110.

References

DfES (2000) *Capability Procedures for Teachers* (0125/2000). London: DfES.

DfES (2002) *Child Protection: Preventing Unsuitable People from Working with Children and Young Persons in the Education Service* (0278/2002). London: DfES.

DfES (2002) *School Teachers' Pay and Conditions Document*. London: DfES (renewed annually).

Finance

Lynn Cousins

In law, the governing body, as a corporate body, is responsible for all money received by the school. This includes the core budget, funding from the DfES, grants, bursaries, gifts and donations made by parents, community members or companies and so on. All money is held on trust by the governing body and you must take measures to manage it efficiently and wisely in order to raise standards of education for the children in the school.

Income

The school's income comes primarily from allocated funding and is supported by income from grants, lettings and charges for school activities. In addition, most schools will be involved in fundraising at some level.

As governors you should

- plan to spend the money from the fair funding formula according to the needs of the school
- plan to spend all of the Standards Fund money according to the guidelines given for that particular year
- plan to raise additional funds when you have identified specific projects
- plan to raise additional funds to supplement basic spending needs if necessary
- plan to retain some of the fair funding formula budget for future needs, planned or as a contingency fund if at all possible
- set out how you intend to balance out any deficit you may have incurred, in the next year's budget.

To do all of this you need to have policies that show

- you have planned ways to monitor the spending to ensure that it is used to benefit all of the children and to fulfil the school's aims of raising standards
- your rationale and systems for raising additional income for the school.

You also need a school improvement plan, or an Ofsted action plan, to show how you intend to raise standards and what the plans will cost to implement. In addition you will need budget plans showing

- how you intend to spend the money in the coming year
- a long-term budget outline to show your spending trends over the next three to five years
- budget updates for each month to monitor trends.

Allocated funding

Allocated funding, often referred to as the core budget or the delegated budget, for the school, comes from two sources. These are

- money delegated by the LEA through the fair funding formula
- Standards Fund money.

Money delegated by the LEA

The money from the LEA is raised from a combination of local government taxation (council tax) and central government grants. The amount of the central government grant to the LEA is based on indicators, which include

- the number of children within the different age groups

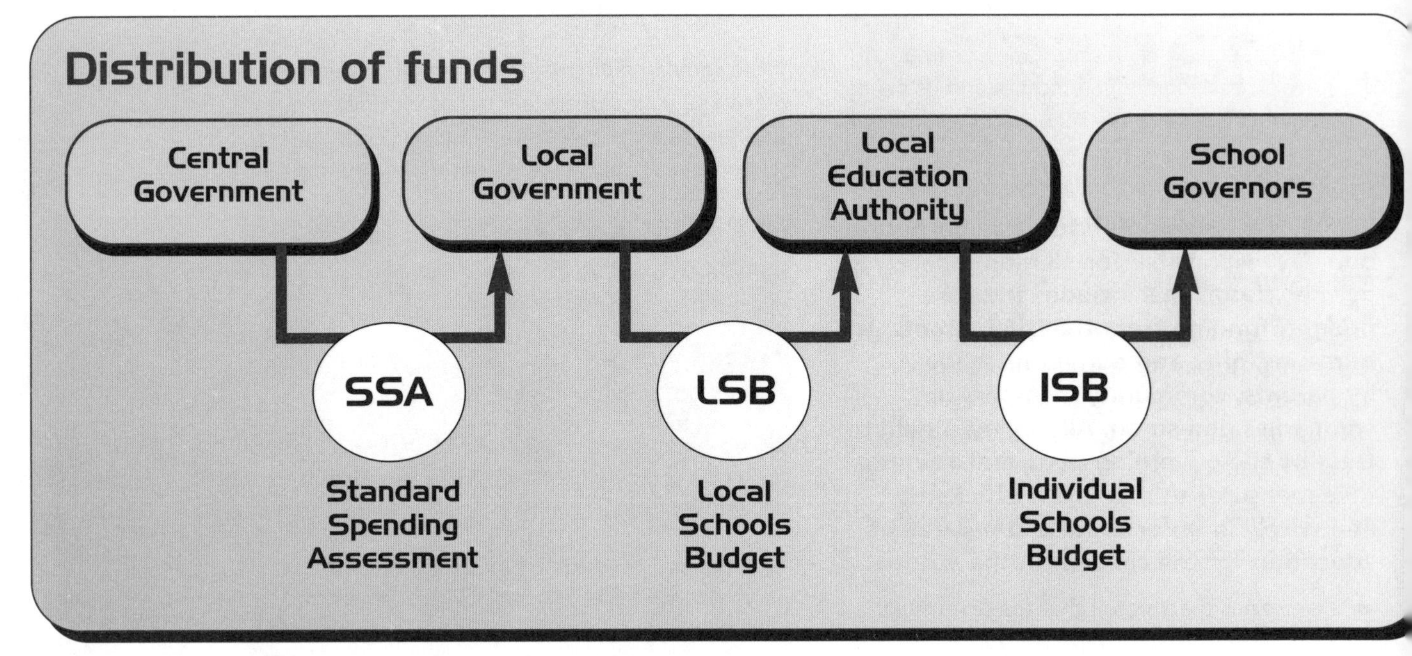

- the distribution of those children across the area
- the socio-economic situation in which those children live
- the area costs.

The figure arrived at is the amount the central government allocates for education to each of the local councils. This amount, the Standard Spending Allowance (SSA), is usually made known to the local authority in early December. Then the local council members decide how much of its total revenue of the council is actually going to delegate to education. This is known as the Local Schools Budget (LSB). It may be less than the SSA or more. The Audit Commission (Audit Commission, 2000 para 87) found that although there is some variation across the country in the amount delegated, the figures are generally quite close.

The LEA decides how much money it's going to delegate directly to schools and how much it needs to retain to fund the five areas for which it remains responsible (non-school activities, strategic management, access, school improvement and special educational needs). The total amount to be delegated to schools is known as the Individual Schools Budget (ISB).

The system of 'fair funding' was introduced in April 1999. This is based on the principles of funding schools according to their needs. A formula is drawn up by each individual LEA, according to a scheme approved by the Secretary of State for Education. Details of the formula will have been discussed at meetings with headteachers and governors. The formula varies between authorities. The LEA then sets a provisional budget for each school based on this formula.

This budget is delegated to the governing body.

Information that has a major influence on the amount of money that the school receives relates to

- the children, according to the data submitted in the annual school census in January (often referred to as Form 7)
- the building, using information from the asset management plan.

For more about asset management plans, see Chapter 8, 'Premises'.

The formula will relate to factors such as

- the number and age of children in the school
- the number of children with special educational needs in the school, or places held specifically for them
- the number of children with English as an additional language
- problems of social deprivation in the area served by the school
- whether the school has a nursery class
- the size of the building (remember to inform the authorities if you extend your teaching space as this will affect your income for the following year)
- the condition of the building – whether, for example, it is on a split site
- whether the school is designated as a 'small school' because of the number of children it can admit.

The provisional or indicative budget share figures are usually sent to schools in January. With the headteacher you can use this information to start making calculations about your next year's budget. School budgets run with the financial year – that is, from 1 April to 31 March. You can make decisions about the spending of this money according to your own knowledge of your school and its needs. This money belongs to the school and as governors you can agree to carry forward some of the money, to fund a long-term project or for future maintenance requirements, and so on.

Standards Fund money

Standards Fund money is directly regulated by the government to pay for items on the national agenda based on government initiatives. It includes specific grants from the government and local matched funding. The government

- determines the broad areas that will receive standards money
- determines the amount that the LEAs must contribute if they wish to take up the available money
- audits the way in which the LEA distributes this between schools
- receives accounts from individual schools on how they spend the money.

Some grants are paid direct to the school and the LEA doesn't have any influence on the actual amount received by each school.

Other government grants are supplements, through matched funding, to what the LEA allocates to particular items. For example, it may be that for every £1000 of its budget the LEA is willing to designate for classroom support, the government will allocate a further £3000 for the authority to hand to individual schools. All of this money has to be spent on the provision of classroom support. It is distributed to schools by the LEA on the basis of need. It is not a flat payment to each school.

With the headteacher, you have to plan to use the Standards Fund money according to the criteria set by the DfES. These change each year. This money cannot be carried forward in the same way as the formula-funded part of the school's income. It must be spent and accounted for by the end of August after the end of the financial year in which it was allocated. So money allocated in April of any year must be spent by August the following year. These arrangements are always liable to change.

Additional funding

Governors are also able to generate additional funding for the school. This includes income from letting the school premises (see Chapter 8), charging for school activities (see Chapter 2, 'The curriculum'), grants from government or other sources, bursaries, donations, sponsorship from local businesses and the many activities for local fundraising in the school community.

Policies for additional funding

There should be discussion among the governors to determine your corporate approach to fundraising. This can be a major source of income for many schools. It can also be time consuming and have serious legal implications. There are risks as well as benefits to be considered. In writing a policy you should commit time to thinking about some of the issues surrounding fundraising.

It's good practice to have a policy that clearly states your rationale. This includes

- why you intend to raise additional funds for the school – promoting the school community, social benefits, specific long-term plans
- what you believe the funds should be used for, in general terms – extras, luxuries, to support the core budget and pay for basic equipment
- who will take responsibility – you may have to take the lead in some areas that need to be dealt with by the legal trustees of the school, while parent associations can take responsibility for other aspects.

How much time can you as governors give to this? There are many tasks that you undertake on behalf of the school, which you cannot delegate. These must be your priority.

Could you be criticised for allowing the government and the LEA to opt out of adequate funding of education if you shore up the system and buy basic requirements for your school?

Is the school financially well managed? Have you monitored your expenditure to make sure that there is no wastage, nor any inappropriate spending patterns?

Have you exhausted LEA grants and other official sources of income? Within the policy you also need to include a section about charging for school activities.

Charging for activities

You cannot levy any charges unless you have first written a policy, which has to be ratified at a meeting of the full governing body, and made its details known to parents. There are regulations about charging for activities. Your policy does not have to be exactly the same as the one produced by the LEA, but it must adhere to the principles of the law.

You can charge for the following.

- Activities that take place outside school hours if they are not a necessary part of the National Curriculum or religious education.

- Individual music tuition, or for music tuition of up to four children in a group. Exemptions to this are detailed in the *Guide to the Law for School Governors* (DfES, 2001a).
- Board and lodgings on residential visits.
- Visits that take place out of school hours or where more than half of the time is out of school session time. Check the *Guide* for details, as this can become quite complicated to work out and there are limitations attached.
- The charge can include an allowance to cover the cost of staffing the activity, as long as you have a written contract or letter with the member of staff defining the service that they will give on that occasion.

You cannot charge for the following.

- Any trips or visits made during the school day, or visits to the school by touring theatre groups, musicians, historical characters, etc. You can only ask for voluntary contributions towards the cost of these. Any money raised must not exceed the actual costs involved in the activity.
- Passengers other than the staff, children and parents for travelling in the school's own minibus.

Within the policy you should include

- details about each of the areas for which you could charge
- details about the level of support for those who can't pay and the criteria for this
- who will administer it and make the decision
- who will be the contact person for parents and carers seeking financial help
- who will pay the subsidy – school funds, curriculum budget, PTA funds.

You should also include a statement about voluntary contributions and how payment or non-payment could affect the activity. For example, if a certain percentage of children do not contribute the activity will have to be cancelled. Or all activities planned as part of the curriculum will be paid for by the PTA funds up to a given total per annum. Or all activities will be funded 50/50 by the PTA and from curriculum funds. Children in receipt of free school meals will not be expected to pay for activities held in school hours.

A summary of the policy on charging for school activities should appear in the school brochure or prospectus so that all parents are aware of the conditions.

For more about charging for school activities, see Chapter 2, 'The curriculum'.

Lettings

In the policy you can outline the arrangements you have in place for the use of the school premises by community members in the form of lettings. This will include who can use the premises, and when. This will be decided by the full governing body or by a premises committee. The finance committee will decide about charges.

What will you charge for the use of the school premises? Most LEAs will have guidelines for you to use. You need to consider

- any costs incurred, such as heating, lighting and power, and cleaning
- security and caretaking arrangements and costs.

Before proceeding, you need to discuss the effect of the use on the day-to-day management of the school. For example, overuse of playing fields could mean that the school fails to provide facilities of the expected quality, or childcare in the hall after school may prevent rehearsals for a school production or some clubs being organised.

If there is a lot of community use, you may need to appoint a second caretaker to cover the hours after school. You will need to look at the financial implications. As well as having another person to pay, you may also need to upgrade your existing caretaker to a level where they can supervise this second caretaker. For occasional use you may be able to pay your existing caretaker overtime.

Administrative time may need to be increased if there is a substantial amount of use. You will also need systems for contracts, and arrangements for charging, for invoicing payments and collecting debts. You will need to provide a pricing system based on actual costs for different areas of the school, by set numbers of people at certain times.

You must cover your costs. You can vary the charges so that one group subsidises another, but you may not subsidise activities from the school's delegated budget. Legally, income from lettings belongs to the LEA, but most have arrangements that allow the school to keep any income.

For more about lettings, see Chapter 8, 'Premises'.

Parents' associations

Any parents' association attached to your school will have its own written constitution. In the policy you can include a short section detailing what you as governors have done to make sure that all activities connected with fundraising are complying with the legal requirements. Most schools have a steady income raised by the parents through numerous activities over the school year.

Any funds raised this way, or goods purchased from this money, become the legal responsibility of the governing body. It is your duty to make sure that

- any promotion clearly states the intended use of the money
- all monies raised are spent as defined in the promotion
- all donated items are properly used and maintained
- all items, donated or purchased, are recorded in such a way that they can be distinguished from items provided by the LEA or bought from the school's budget
- all amounts raised are banked separately until such time as they are spent.

Other sources of additional income tend to be one-off gifts or grants linked to some particular development that the school is involved in, or they take the form of partnerships with local businesses. The rationale for these will come from your original statements within the policy if, and when, you decide to approach fundraising in this way.

Sponsorship

Partnerships with local businesses can take two forms, namely

1. money, time or goods donated by the business as part of their charitable giving
2. a business deal, whereby the company must receive benefits in return for their giving.

Before entering into a business partnership you need to discuss a number of questions.

- How will the children benefit?
- How could it affect standards for the children?
- Will it offend any of the parents in our community?
- Will it be time-consuming to administer?
- Are there any ethical issues to do with the company and its work methods or business dealings?
- Will we be used as a marketing tool by the company?
- Are we unofficially endorsing products?
- What benefits will the school gain from management expertise from within the company?

If you decide to go ahead, you need to take legal advice (usually available from the LEA) to make sure that you and the company act within the law. Your local Chamber of Commerce will also be able to offer you advice on companies who may be interested in setting up a partnership with your school. There are often established groups linking local businesses with education.

Grants

Many charities will support special ventures with grants. Each one has its own criteria for you to meet. These can include

- matched funding
- evidence of sufficient funds, or plans to fund a project after the charity has paid for its set-up costs
- links with the local community
- development of the local area.

Charities may give

- set-up fees
- repayment on receipt of paid accounts
- fixed amounts
- enough to cover the full costs.

Applying to charities is time-consuming and complex. Although some charities will only allocate gifts to governing bodies, as the legal trustees of the school's money you may choose to delegate this task. Further information is available from pfp publishing in *Solutions: Raising Additional Income*.

Setting the budget

The DfES has published guidelines, The School Finance Pack (DfES 2001b), for all schools to follow when setting their budget. These are available free of charge from the department by phoning their orders line.

Since April 2002 all schools have been coding their budget items under the same headings. This is to make it easier to

- compare your school's spending patterns with other similar schools and match spending patterns with standards achieved in end of key stage assessments
- provide Ofsted inspectors with the sort of financial data they need, so that they can comment on the school's ability to provide value for money.

There are more details about this later in the chapter, in the section devoted to 'Value for money'. The specific budget headings are listed in the DfES pack, and are referred to as Consistent Financial Reporting (CFR).

The headteacher and chair of the finance committee can draw up some provisional budgets for governors to debate and eventually agree. As you consider these budgets, the issues you need to take note of include previous budgets, the current needs of the school, recommendations from Ofsted inspectors and school improvement planning.

Previous budgets

Look at past budgets and how well they worked – or didn't work.

- Did we have to move large amounts of money from one budget heading to another? (This is known as 'viring'.) Where to? Where from?
- Why? Was it an unusual one-off emergency situation or have the school's needs changed dramatically in some areas?
- Have we ended the year with a considerable under-spend in one budget area?

Current needs of the school

Challenge existing spending patterns.

- Have our school priorities changed?
- Curriculum and office needs have changed as technology gains a more powerful place in our lives.
- Are there ways of reducing our energy commitments?
- Can we set an example in responding to global issues?
- Are we committing a fair percentage of our income to staff training, maintenance, music education, etc?
- How do our spending patterns compare with other schools in our sort of situation?

There is 'benchmarking' information available to help you to work this out. See the 'Value for money' section.

You may find that you don't need to change the pattern of the previous years, but it is still good practice to raise the questions every three or four years. Don't become complacent.

Carry out an assessment of the needs of the school for each of the areas identified in the Standards Fund.

If you have separate committees taking responsibility for premises, security and/or health and safety, they can carry out a risk assessment by walking around the school and identifying any areas of concern. For curriculum needs, ask the teachers who coordinate each area to carry out an audit of their training and resource needs. Ask the headteacher to carry out, or organise, audits of the needs of any other area where money has been allocated by the government.

Use all this information to determine priorities for the coming year's spending.

Recommendations from Ofsted inspectors

If your school has been inspected in the last three years, you may well be working towards the targets agreed in your action plan. In your next inspection these will be investigated, so make sure that you budget for them. Some issues may have been raised that didn't form part of your existing budget and you may have had to rearrange your plans to accommodate them. There should be some extra

School improvement plan
TARGET. To raise the level of boys' reading in KS2 national tests from x to y

Action	Costs				
	Resources	Staff/Supply	Training	TOTAL	Budget code
More non-fiction texts in classroom libraries	£100 per class x 8 classes	£0	£0	£800	E19
Increase amount of fiction for boys/male-oriented texts in school library	£300	£0	£0	£300	E19
Class teachers to read a broader range of texts to the whole class	£0	£0	£0	£0	n/a
Training for all staff about preferences held by boys, suitable resources, and approaches to engage boys in reading	£0	£500	£500	£1000	E09
TOTAL	£1,100	£500	£500	£2,100	

These amounts represent only a part of the money that will be included under these headings, but this amount should be given a priority as it is part of the school's identified targets for improvement.

money available to you to assist with this. If you have had to change things part-way through a financial year, remember to take this into account when you evaluate the budget and prepare your next one.

School improvement plan

The school improvement plan (SIP) has a pivotal role in the ongoing development of the school and the need to raise standards. As governors you should make sure that there is a link between the targets set in the SIP, the projected costs of achieving those targets and the money delegated to those areas within the budget.

An example is given on page 118.

All of these areas should be debated as you consider the options presented in the provisional budget plans. Your aim is to spend the money wisely, so that the children in the school will benefit in sound educational ways, and to make sure that the school is a safe and secure place for those who work in it.

Planning your expenditure

See the table on page 120. If you have decided that it would be a valuable exercise to challenge your school's spending patterns, use a table like this one. Photocopy the table onto A3 paper to allow plenty of space within each box.

Fill in your own items in the first row.
Then start to add the details of your projected costs. Use it as a wish list in the first instance but be practical – you don't want the exercise to be a waste of time.

Once it is complete, make a copy for each member at the meeting. You can now discuss where you may need to make alterations so that your budget will balance. You may not know the amount you are going to receive in the Standards Fund until very close to the date when you need to be agreeing the final budget. You will have to rely on figures from past years or from hints picked up by the headteacher at meetings.

School improvement plan

List targets, and for each one, fill in the projected costs. This is the area where you can make adjustments to your planned expenditure most easily.

The plan may contain some actions from an inspection that you must work on. This may be the area most easily funded by the Standards Fund money, because some of the work here tends to reflect government initiatives.

School organisation and administrative costs

These areas should be the focus for long-term planning. Employment law is complex, and you would need to take advice from human resource personnel if, for example, you needed to make a teacher redundant. Taking on extra staff means a long-term financial commitment, so this also needs careful thought and discussion.

Maximum class sizes in Key Stage 1 are set by legal requirement and the cost of an extra teacher can be supported by direct grants from the LEA in the short term. Take advice if your numbers increase to give more than 30 children for any class in this age group.

Premises

List all contracts, services and energy costs, and repairs budget. Try not to cut back on this expenditure, unless you can clearly see that you have been over-funding it in past years.

Repairs and maintenance jobs will only get worse and become more expensive to fix at a later date if they are neglected. It is generally cheaper to maintain than to replace equipment. Some jobs remain the responsibility of the LEA, so check with your local authority to find out who does what.

This is an area where you may need to spend less but save more to cover anticipated future costs. For example, you may have recently fitted new carpets throughout the school. How long will they last? You may decide to save towards their replacement costs.

Educational resources

Define your needs according to key stages or by curriculum areas. These expenditures may overlap the plans in your SIP. Make sure you only account for them once as you go through this exercise.

If you have a shortfall in your budget, this may be an area where you can easily make some cuts. Check suppliers for bargains – ask around the local businesses or parent contacts for paper and card offcuts, etc.

You could divide necessary resources such as paint, pencils and exercise books from those things that you can manage without. If this is an area where you need to consider cutbacks, ask the headteacher to look into this and provide you with a realistic figure. You don't need to worry about the details of the spending.

If you still have a serious shortfall, or will have to forgo some exciting new development in order to balance your budget, you have one more course open to you. You can raise the money. Details of how you can do this are in the section 'Additional funding' earlier in this chapter.

Planning your expenditure

	Teachers	Support staff	Staff training	Classroom resources	Premises	Admin	Other (identity)	TOTAL
SIP								
School organisation								
Premises								
Admin costs								
Ed. resources								

Checklist for setting the budget

Staffing costs These use about 80 per cent of the whole budget share and need careful, detailed calculation. Your school's secretary will be able to project the figures using the office computer program. You need to account for

- ❑ numbers of teachers, classroom and special needs support staff, lunchtime staff based on projected number of children in the school and by using the school organisation plan the headteacher will have prepared.
- ❑ level of office/administrative staff you need
- ❑ number of caretaking and cleaning staff needed
- ❑ pay rises (April – cost of living, Sept – incremental)
- ❑ pay awards for performance management – threshold payments, discretionary pay awards (Sept)
- ❑ any changes to the employment on-costs.

Unavoidable expenditure There are a number of items which cannot be ignored and these should be the next priority. These include

- ❑ health and safety
- ❑ insurance
- ❑ free school meals, if this has been delegated to the school
- ❑ repayment of any deficit
- ❑ loans and leasing agreements.

Premises costs This includes items that are contractual, and therefore at a fixed rate, and other items, such as energy, repairs and decoration costs, where you can be flexible in the amount of money you commit.

- ❑ Repairs and maintenance. Some of this will be contractual, some in the buy-back services, and some will be of your own choosing. If you are struggling to set a budget, itemise these so that you can plan your spending.
- ❑ Grounds maintenance.
- ❑ Refuse disposal.
- ❑ Energy costs (itemise according to your usage: gas, oil, electricity, water, solid fuel). Remember to take account of inflation.

Remaining money You can now allocate the rest of your budget share, along with your Standards Fund money according to

- ❑ administrative costs – equipment and stationery, etc.
- ❑ SIP targets
- ❑ government initiatives
- ❑ staff and governor development and training needs
- ❑ resource needs – stationery, consumables, books, ICT and other equipment
- ❑ contingency budget.

Checklist for long-term financial planning

Your aim is to decide how large a balance you should plan for.

You can use your balance to

- ❑ cover the school against contingencies or emergencies in the short term
- ❑ sustain current levels of expenditure, staffing, etc. when your numbers and your budget have been reduced
- ❑ pay for identified needs including repairs, redecoration or refurbishment
- ❑ complete a planned development over the coming years.

Using the planning sheet

On the planning sheet overleaf, write in details of your known planned future spending needs. For example, an increase in the number of teachers as you anticipate increased numbers of children due to a change in the school catchment area, or the building of a new estate nearby. Or a decrease in the number of teachers due to falling rolls or a change in the age of transfer. Or details from a rolling programme of redecoration that the premises committee has organised. In each category note down what you envisage needing to spend.

Categorise your spending as

- ❑ additional unavoidable expenditure
- ❑ potential savings
- ❑ only if additional funds are available.

Remember

You can only save money which is surplus to requirements. You are duty bound to spend your budget for the benefit of the children in the school. Do not save money without good reason.

Long-term financial plan

Details and anticipated costs

	Year 1	Year 2	Year 3	Year 4	Year 5
Staffing levels – Management – Teaching – Support – Lunchtime – Caretaking – Cleaning					
Repairs and maintenance, including redecoration and replacement					
Resources – ICT – Other					

For more about setting the budget, see the 'Checklist for setting the budget', 'Checklist for long-term financial planning' and 'Long-term financial plan' on pages 121–122.

Monitoring the budget

Monitoring the school budget is one of the governing body's key roles. As holders of public money, you are accountable to the auditors and to Ofsted inspectors. You must be able to show that the money you have received, from whatever source, has been spent efficiently and that you can demonstrate that the school gives value for money.

Monitoring the budget is, however, a shared responsibility. In all financial matters it's good practice to have more than one party involved, each taking care of one part, but each one's responsibilities overlapping with another's. This practice reduces the risk of serious mistakes.

Financial policy

Your financial policy could deal with such things as

- areas of responsibility
- day-to-day control systems
- reporting systems.

Areas of responsibility

The school should have a policy defining areas of responsibility, agreed by the governing body. A simple and effective system is as follows.

- **Headteacher** – executive tasks, such as viring money up to an agreed amount. This amount, stated as money or as a percentage of the budget allocation for each area, and any constraints should be clearly stated to avoid confusion at a later date.
- **School secretary or bursar** – administrative tasks, such as checking the payments of invoices, keeping records of payments and income.
- **Governors' finance committee** – monitoring that things are going according to plan.

Day-to-day control systems

There should also be agreed systems for the day-to-day financial management within the school. This is the responsibility of the head, but you should be aware of what controls the headteacher has put in place for everyday transactions such as purchasing, banking procedures and dealing with income. These could be explained in the policy. Good practice is to have different people doing different aspects of the ordering of goods. For example, the headteacher agrees orders, the secretary or bursar places the order, a third person (additional office personnel, a classroom support person or the deputy head) opens and checks orders as they arrive in school.

Reporting systems

Include details explaining how you will report financial matters, when these reports can be expected and who will take responsibility for writing them. Reports will be needed from

- subject coordinators to the headteacher
- the headteacher to the finance committee
- the finance committee to the governing body
- the full governing body to the LEA, auditors, Ofsted inspectors, the DfES and parents.

Decide what information will be required at each level of reporting and the format it will take. Tables and charts are often easier to read than prose. If you have a prepared format it will also give consistent information, which is more useful when you want to draw comparisons.

It's good practice to have more than one party involved with overlapping responsibilities ... this practice reduces the risk of serious mistakes

The monthly printout

Before you can monitor the spending, you have to know how and where the money is being spent. To do this you need to see a monthly printout of the school's financial position. This information is held on the school's computer and can be accessed by the head at any time. It's good practice for this information to be shared with the governors, and specifically

- with the chair of the finance committee each month
- with members of the finance committee whenever they meet
- with all governors at full meetings of the governing body.

All financial transactions are entered into the office computer. The monthly printout will show

- the amount you budgeted under each heading
- the total amount you have already committed from that heading (this should be based on orders placed and invoices raised, rather than the actual receipt or payment of money)
- the amount you have left to spend under each heading.

An example is given in the table on page 124.

Some printouts show projected spending. They can show, for example, the outstanding commitments for salaries, for energy payments or monthly commitments for maintenance or leasing contracts and how they will affect the budget plan.

Sample section of a monthly printout

	Budget	Committed	Remaining
Office costs			
Stationery	£300	£178	£122
Maintaining equip.	£1000	£550	£450
Postage	£200	£65	£135
Phones, incl. ICT	£1000	£750	£250
Total	**£2500**	**£1543**	**£957**

Others show the variance between the projected and the actual spending. These can be positive or deficit variances, but need a response. This is the duty of the headteacher in the first instance. Within the limits and constraints agreed by the governors, and written down clearly and specifically in the financial policy, the head can vire money between sections of the budget in order to maintain an overall balance. At the next finance committee meeting the head should explain this to governors so that you remain in touch with how the school's spending is progressing. Any significant variance will need governor debate on the way forward. This may have been an exceptional circumstance or it may need further investigation at the time you start to agree the next budget. Remember to take account of any virements, and the reasons for them, when you come to set the new budget.

According to the Audit Commission (2000, para 22), it is best practice to use the most straightforward of possible printouts in the quest for clarity. You need to be provided with usable information – not to be confused with obscure technical data. If necessary, more complex printouts can then be used to investigate areas giving concern.

The budget profile

You should complete a budget profile for your school as you plan the budget. It will then become a useful tool for monitoring the progress of your spending throughout the year.

As a template for planning your budget, you can use copies of the 'Budget profile format' on page 126.

You could make a copy for 'income' if you have income spread out over the year, for example from lettings or sponsorship.

Use the copy of the budget profile format to plan your expenditure.

- Place the budget codes in the first column.
- Add details of known expenditure dates.
- Quarterly bills can be estimated on previous year's budgets.
- Direct debits can be accurately placed.
- Maintenance contracts, leasing arrangements and insurances will all have due dates you can use.
- Staffing costs can be calculated on the school's office computer program.
- Other expenditure such as purchasing stationery for the next school year can be estimated and placed on the profile.

The budget profile will show how the income and expenditure should occur throughout the year. Use this alongside the monthly printout to show whether spending is going according to plan. You will be able to see whether there is any variance between what you expected to happen and what is actually happening.

Together, the printouts of actual spending and the profiles of planned spending will help you to see

- that things are going to plan
- where there have been some unexpected bills which could lead to a problem in one or other budget area later in the year (with this knowledge you can start to plan ahead to pre-empt difficulties before they are upon you)
- the balance of spending over the year
- areas where you have under- or over-estimated the costs
- where corrective measures have been taken.

All of this information will inform your decisions when you come to agree the budget for the next financial year.

Value for money

Having checked that the actual spending follows the agreed plan, the more difficult, but very important, task is to ensure that the spending has given value for money.

Budget profile

	Apr	May	June	July	Aug	Sept	Oct	Nov	Dec	Jan	Feb	Mar
E01 Teaching staff £134,000	£10,000	£10,000	£10,000	£10,000	£10,000	£12,000	£12,000	£12,000	£12,000	£12,000	£12,000	£12,000
E16 Energy – gas £1,100	£500	£0	£0	£200	£0	£0	£50	£0	£0	£350	£0	£0
E19 Learning resources £1,450	£250	£0	£0	£800	£0	£200	£0	£100	£0	£0	£0	£100
E20 ICT learning resources £1,775	£100	£0	£1,200	£100	£0	£175	£100	£0	£0	£100	£0	£0
E23 Other insurance premiums £1,400	£600	£0	£0	£0	£0	£800	£0	£0	£0	£0	£0	£0

Budget profile format

Budget heading code	Apr	May	June	July	Aug	Sept	Oct	Nov	Dec	Jan	Feb	Mar

There are three main questions.

1 Are we managing our assets wisely?

2 Are we spending wisely and is our budget cost-effective?

3 Are there real, even if non-quantitative, educational benefits from our spending?

Asset management

The governing body is ultimately responsible for the good management of all the school's assets, financial and physical. You should make sure that

- there is an inventory of all assets
- there are procedures for disposing of assets when necessary
- all buildings are secured against the risk of damage
- there are arrangements in case of claims made against the school, including any legal costs incurred
- there is a school policy for recovering costs of accidental and non-accidental damage to the school's assets by children, staff or any other person on the premises
- there are arrangements for controlling the school's consumable stock (books, stationery, educational equipment, and so on)
- there are maintenance agreements in place.

It is not your responsibility to carry out all of these actions, but to make sure that there are policies and systems in place, that the responsibilities are delegated appropriately and that they are being followed efficiently.

For more about asset management, see Chapter 8, 'Premises'.

Cost-effectiveness

It's worth considering your spending in terms of cost-effectiveness. Think about whether you are spending more than you need to. Could you get better value for your money from other providers?

With regard to **energy**, consider the following questions.

- Are you wasteful with your use of light and heat? There is a balance to be found between enough light to be safe and to protect the eyesight of the children and the staff, and the wastage when lights are left on in unused areas of the school.
- Are there cheaper suppliers of energy?
- Can you get a reduction in costs by using direct debit services?
- Have you considered using low-energy bulbs?
- Is heat escaping through ill-fitting doors and windows?
- What is the state of the draught-proofing in the roof space?

Turn your attention to **resources**.

- Are you using suppliers who give best value for money? Consider quality, reliability and hidden costs such as postage and packing.
- Is your stock well managed? Could you improve storage arrangements to prevent damage to equipment or supplies?
- Do you recycle material where appropriate?
- Could you bulk-buy some items and store them for later use?
- Are cleaning materials, paper towels, etc., similarly well chosen and used sensibly?

The headteacher or a teacher governor would be the best person to look into these issues with the staff.

For **services**, when you are looking at the various options available (whether to use your local LEA, or change to another LEA or outside companies) you could pose some of these questions.

- Do other providers know your particular situation well?
- Do other providers have a vested interest in supporting your school?
- Who is going to take responsibility for checking the commercial viability of the service providers available?
- Are these other providers available if you need to talk to them face to face, or after office hours? Where are they based?

Educational benefits

Benefits to staff

- Do staff have the right tools for the job?
- Are they well supported by classroom support workers and professional development training?

Money spent here can raise morale and make staff feel regarded and valued. This will help to create a positive working atmosphere. You could use the opportunity of a visit to the school to ask the staff about their needs in terms of additional resources. Talk about these with the headteacher, bearing in mind the questions raised earlier about the cost-effectiveness of resources. If it's agreed that money should be allocated to address some of these needs, you can give serious consideration to increasing the amount of the money that you budget for educational resources, staff training, and so on.

> The governing body is ultimately responsible for the good management of all the school's assets, financial and physical

Benefits to children

- Is the school a safe and secure place for them?
- Is the building bright and welcoming?
- Are the classrooms warm, clean and tidy?
- Is the equipment appropriate for today's curriculum?
- Is the playground a stimulating area or is it a threatening environment, bleak, cold and dull?
- Are the children achieving as they should be?

There are several tools you can use to answer this last question. They include

1 the school improvement plan

2 end of key stage assessment results

3 comparative data or benchmarking.

The school improvement plan

In the school improvement plan you should have targets for raising standards of achievement in some key areas of the curriculum. The headteacher will be able to provide you with information about the success rate. Ask yourselves these questions.

- Did we reach our targets?
- Were the targets too low or too high?
- Did we spend money according to the plan? Or more than we planned? Or less?
- Where do we go from here?
- Do we need to spend more money on repeating the strategy? Do we need a new strategy? Have we solved the problem once and for all?

End of key stage assessment results

The headteacher will be able to talk you through the results of these assessments. They vary year on year according to the particular group of children involved, their ages, their gender and their special needs. Taking account of this natural variation, there are several questions to ask.

- Could we realistically improve on these results?
- Are the staffing levels as good as they could be?
- Should we be providing more support from suitably qualified classroom assistants?
- Would homework clubs be a useful addition to the school?
- Are resources adequate?

Comparative data or benchmarking

This is another useful tool for evaluating your spending in terms of educational value.

The Autumn Package and the PANDA report will give you figures that allow you to compare your school with others of a similar size and community. You can, for example, compare their spending on classroom support and assessment results with yours. Does increasing one lead to an increase in the other? It is worth devoting some of your committee time to this exercise as it will help you to formulate decisions about your spending patterns in relation to other schools and to the educational results you achieve.

The Audit Commission has set up a useful website, www.schools.audit-commission.gov.uk/schoolfinance, which allows you to key in information about your own school anonymously and it will provide you with charts and graphs to show how your data compares with those of similar schools.

Financial accountability

As a governing body you have a duty to show various other bodies that you are managing the school well. This includes reporting about financial matters to the LEA, parents and Ofsted inspectors.

Data will also be collected by the DfES and the Audit Commission for the purpose of benchmarking and in an attempt to maximise the benefits of good financial management for all schools.

Reporting to the LEA

The LEA has the right to attend governors' meetings and any committee meeting with financial matters on the agenda.

The LEA also has the right to suspend the delegated budget if it has evidence of mismanagement or gross incompetence in the handling of the school's budget share. In such cases the LEA must give written notice of their intentions, detailing any allegations and identifying the grounds for the suspension. The governing body has the right to appeal to the Secretary of State within two months. The LEA must review the suspension before the start of each financial year. The suspension may be revoked. If not, the governors can appeal again. During the suspension the governors may be allowed to make some financial decisions within boundaries set by the LEA.

Primary schools are normally audited by their LEA every four years, although there is a wide variation in practice (Audit Commission, 2000, para 51). The

Financial information for the governors' report to parents

April 20___ to March 20___

	INCOME	
Carry forward Budget share Standards Fund Other: – Grants – Fundraising by PTA – Lettings – School activities – Bank interest		
TOTAL AVAILABLE BUDGET		
	EXPENDITURE	
	Actual	**Per child**
Staffing costs Premises costs Energy costs Administrative costs Resources: – ICT – Other Other costs Contingency fund		
TOTAL		

Comments

Our policy towards financial priorities

Intended use of our contingency fund

Plan to pay back any deficit

information gathered from this audit is fed back to the governing body. You should then respond to any recommendations in order to improve the financial management of your school.

Reporting to parents

The governors' annual report to parents must include a financial statement for the last complete financial year. Parents can discuss this at the meeting. Governors must answer reasonable requests for information from individual parents or staff members.

There is a template of 'Financial information for the governors' report to parents' on page 129.

Reporting to Ofsted inspectors

An Ofsted inspection will include scrutiny of how well the school is managed financially, to make sure that resources are well used for the benefit of the children. Inspectors will be interested in policies and practice and will need to see evidence of these.

Plan your committee meeting agendas so that you regularly review your policies and strategies. Minute any actions or reports that deal with monitoring the spending in the school. Minute any financial decisions you take as a committee, or that you refer to the full governing body, and any decision taken there.

Keep evidence that you use all available data to monitor your own spending and that you have compared it to spending in other similar schools in your search for best value.

References

The Audit Commission (2000) *Money Matters. School Funding and Resource Management National Report*. London: The Audit Commission.

DfES (2001a) *A Guide to the Law for School Governors – Community Schools (Primary)*. London DfES.

DfES (2001b) *The School Finance Pack. Promoting Benchmarking and Accountability in Schools*. London: DfES.

NAGM (2001) Paper No. 45: *The Financial Responsibilities of Governors*. Fifth edition. Birmingham: National Association of Governors and Managers.

NAGM (1999) Paper No. 36: *Governors and Fundraising*. Fourth edition. Birmingham: National Association of Governors and Managers.

Premises

Craig Shaw

Most people feel more comfortable dealing with matters about which they have some practical understanding or personal opinion, rather than with complex issues that require specialist, professional input. Many a governing body meeting gets bogged down with issues about the drains or a new colour scheme, when governors could more valuably be devoting their time to matters that will more directly improve educational standards for the children. Coupled with this, you may be, like many other governors, unclear about your responsibilities with regard to premises matters and the relative roles of the governing body and the headteacher.

In September 2000 the then Department for Education and Employment published a guidance document entitled *Roles of Governing Bodies and Head Teachers* (DfEE, 2000). You might find this helpful when you are considering an appropriate allocation of responsibilities. Paragraphs 5 and 6 of this guidance refer to the 1998 School Standards and Framework Act.

> The governing body are to carry out their functions with the aim of taking a largely strategic role in the running of the school. This includes setting up a strategic framework for the school, setting its aims and objectives, setting policies and targets for achieving the objectives, reviewing progress and reviewing the strategic framework in the light of progress.
>
> The headteacher is responsible for the internal organisation, management and control of the school; and for advising on and implementing the governing body's strategic framework. In particular, headteachers need to formulate aims and objectives, policies and targets for the governing body to consider adopting.

Nowhere in any government publication is the relationship between strategic and managerial functions more clearly set out.

Within the guidance booklet is a Decision Planner, which lists some 81 tasks that the governing body should consider. There is a short section on premises, which states that there are four specific tasks. These are

- buildings insurance – the governing body is to seek advice from LEA, diocese or trustees where appropriate
- strategy (including budgeting for repairs, etc.) and asset management plans
- to ensure health and safety issues are met
- to set a charging and remissions policy.

While there are no specific regulations indicating who should carry out the first three of these tasks, the fourth is said to be the responsibility of the governing body as a whole.

The supporting notes to the Decision Planner distinguish the roles of the headteacher and governing body, as summarised in the table below.

The premises committee

All committees must have clear terms of reference, which define their composition, quorum, chairing and clerking, minutes, arrangements for convening meetings and, most importantly, their functions. Members of committees will want to be clear about these matters.

Responsibilities of the headteacher	Responsibilities of the governing body
Control of school premises	
Day-to-day management of the school and charge of who can enter the school premises. To advise the governing body where appropriate.	To control the use of the school premises both during and outside the school day. To decide on what charges to levy where external providers want to use the school premises.
Health and safety	
To comply with the LEA's directions in community and voluntary controlled schools. In voluntary aided and foundation schools to comply with governing body directions.	To prepare a health and safety policy, carry out risk assessments and set up arrangements to manage health and safety in foundation and voluntary aided schools. In community and controlled schools this is the LEA's responsibility.

(Based on DfEE, 2000)

It's a good idea for you to have a premises committee to take responsibility for specific issues. This will help you to make sure that such matters receive appropriate attention but don't intrude unreasonably on the work of the governing body as a whole. When you are determining the functions of a premises committee, you will want to give careful consideration to the overall responsibilities of the headteacher and the governing body.

As the manager of the school, the headteacher should clearly hold the day-to-day responsibilities and should prepare specific proposals for consideration by the premises committee. That committee is likely to have specific delegated responsibilities as indicated below, and will make recommendations on other matters to the whole governing body. It will submit the minutes of its meetings to the full governing body, which will maintain ultimate responsibility and will need to approve the committee's actions and decisions.

It is important that you and your fellow governors understand the nature of your role and don't attempt to influence the day-to-day management of premises matters. However, as individuals, governors and others may have experience, skills and expertise, perhaps because of their own employment. Specialist knowledge can be invaluable and the headteacher may be pleased to use it. Any support you can give in this way will be on a personal basis, rather than in your capacity as a governor.

Responsibilities regarding school premises

There are differences in the extent of the responsibilities of the governing bodies of different types of school.

In community schools

- The LEA owns the land and buildings.
- Capital works are funded by the LEA.
- The governing body pays for repairs and maintenance from its budget share.
- The governing body and the LEA share responsibility for health and safety.
- The governing body controls the use of the premises both during and outside the school day but has to follow any general rules laid down by the LEA.

In voluntary controlled schools

- The school's land and buildings are normally owned by a charitable foundation.
- Capital works are funded by the LEA.
- The governing body pays for repairs and maintenance from its budget share.
- The governing body and the LEA share responsibility for health and safety.
- Unless a trust deed specifies some other arrangement, the governing body controls the use of the premises both during and outside the school day but has to follow any general rules laid down by the LEA.
- The foundation governors decide on the use of the premises on Sundays.

In voluntary aided schools

- The school's land and buildings are normally owned by a charitable foundation.
- Capital works are normally funded by the governing body which may be eligible for grants of up to 85 per cent from the DfES. The LEA may also contribute to capital expenditure and is responsible for providing a new site if the school moves.
- The LEA is responsible for repairs and maintenance to the inside of the school buildings and includes an appropriate sum in the school's budget share.
- The LEA provides and maintains school playing fields and excepted buildings such as caretakers' houses, sports pavilions, medical inspection rooms, kitchen and dining rooms.
- The governing body is responsible for health and safety.
- The governing body controls how the school premises are used both during and outside school hours, unless a trust deed specifies some other arrangement.

In foundation schools

- The school's land and buildings are owned by the governing body or by a charitable foundation.
- Capital works are normally funded by the LEA.
- The governing body pays for repairs and maintenance from its budget share.
- The governing body is responsible for health and safety.
- The governing body controls how the school premises are used both during and outside school hours, unless a trust deed specifies some other arrangement.

Monitoring the premises

To fulfil your responsibilities for the school premises you need to know about its condition and use. To a large extent you can rely on the headteacher to keep you in the picture. The headteacher, in turn, will receive information from the caretaker or site manager and the specialist officers from the LEA.

Everything will be clearer, however, if you have a good knowledge of the premises yourself.

You can get this knowledge partly through your routine visits to the school. As well as looking at lessons and so on, make a point of noting anything specific about the buildings and site – their general condition, how they are used, any safety issues.

You can gather more in-depth information from regular monitoring visits by the premises committee. These visits might take place once a term – or perhaps more frequently if there is some particular issue to be considered. Guided by the headteacher and caretaker or site manager, such visits can be to get an overall view of the school and its general condition. They can also focus on specific matters such as repairs, safety or the use of particular areas. Occasionally – perhaps once a year – the whole governing body might be invited to visit with the premises committee.

Delegation of responsibilities for premises

Headteacher

The following functions might be delegated to the headteacher within overall policies, who would report to the governing body each term.

- To monitor the fabric of the school and to be responsible for day-to-day repairs and maintenance, within the annual budget, taking account of the variation limits set within financial regulations.
- To draw up an annual maintenance programme, for recommendation to the premises committee, taking such professional advice as is deemed necessary.
- To draw up an annual replacement programme for furniture, fittings and equipment for recommendation to the premises committee, taking professional advice as deemed necessary.
- To be responsible for liaison with contractors where work is funded from the school's budget and with the LEA (and foundation, as appropriate) where capital works are funded from central resources.
- To take such urgent premises actions as are required in consultation with the committee chair and, if necessary, the LEA or foundation.
- To be responsible for the arrangements for letting the school premises.
- To be responsible for the day-to-day security of the school premises.
- To be responsible for the day-to-day cleaning, caretaking and catering arrangements on the school premises.
- To be responsible for the day-to-day health and safety arrangements in the school.
- To arrange appropriate insurances in respect of the school premises and contents.

Premises committee

The following responsibilities might be delegated to a premises committee.

- To be jointly responsible, with the finance committee, for determining a policy and scale of charges for the letting of the premises.
- To monitor the operation of the LEA's (or foundation's) Health and Safety Policy Statement in order to safeguard the health and safety of employees, children and visitors.
- To make recommendations for updating the school development plan as it relates to the management of school premises.
- To approve tenders and expenditures within the limits delegated to committees.

Governing body

The following responsibilities might be subject to approval by the governing body.

- To consider recommendations from the headteacher with regard to the annual maintenance and replacement programmes, being those items of expenditure funded from the delegated budget, and to make formal proposals for expenditure.
- To consider improvements and alterations to the school premises that can be met from delegated capital and other resources and to forward proposals to the LEA (or foundation, as appropriate) for consideration and approval.
- To consider, approve or propose amendments to the LEA's asset management plan and to liaise with the LEA on improvements and alterations to school premises that can be met from the authority's resources or government grants.
- To set a school charging and remissions policy.
- To approve tenders and expenditures that exceed the limits delegated to committees within the financial regulations.

Maintenance

As with any buildings, schools need maintenance work on a regular basis. Not only must the structure and fabric of the school be kept in a sound condition, but the overall finish and presentation of the premises is of significant importance to the delivery of effective education and to the sense of belonging of the children and the community.

All local authorities now have asset management plans, which schedule the condition of their buildings and propose significant work that will be necessary over a period of years. As a governing body you will wish to comment on the section of the plan that relates to your school and, once it has been agreed with the LEA, you will wish to use it as a key document for premises considerations. Any planned work at the school that is included in the LEA's asset management plan should also be included within the school development plan, which might include programmes for maintenance, refurbishment and improvement.

Maintenance work is generally described as revenue expenditure. This means that it's met from the budget delegated from the LEA, or from lump sums such as the School Support Grant. School maintenance work can fall into a number of categories.

Cleaning and caretaking

You should consider cleaning and caretaking to be an essential element of your maintenance work. The headteacher will recommend appropriate arrangements for cleaning the school and, as a governing body, you will enter into a contract for this work. There is, of course, a relationship between the level of day-to-day cleaning, the overall condition of the school and the maintenance work needed. This links into caretaking, and schools have many different arrangements for this. At one end of the spectrum, the caretaker is effectively a keyholder, who opens and closes the school, keeps an eye out during after-school activities, and reports any concerns or supplies needed. At the other end of the spectrum, the caretaker acts as a site manager, arranging and supervising services and undertaking such minor maintenance work as is within their abilities. While acceptable arrangements may have been in place for many years, you will want to consider from time to time whether some other arrangement may be beneficial. A more regular presence, for example, may enable vandalism to be dealt with more quickly, minor repairs to be done without delay, and overall maintenance costs to be reduced.

Redecoration

This is an important and ongoing element of the maintenance programme and advice is usually available from the LEA. Some parts of the school will need painting quite regularly – others less frequently. Try to have an ongoing plan for five or more years, which includes the whole of the premises. This ensures that all aspects of the work have been provided for, but also allows for a good relationship to develop with an individual contractor for (say) one complete cycle. In this way the costs can usually be kept under control and the work can be planned for the most appropriate times in the year.

Your LEA might have a maintenance scheme that you can buy into if you wish. If you don't have a long-term plan you may have to use what services you can find, and may have to put up with the inconvenience of work during term time. Whatever approach is used, you should pay close attention to the need for competitive tendering and the principles of best value. For more about best value, see the section on 'Contracts, purchasing and best value' later in this chapter.

Refurbishment

Refurbishment is the replacement of elements of the fabric of the building and its contents. There can be something of an overlap between refurbishment and improvement, as one generally brings about the other, but for the sake of a definition, you can think of refurbishment as a like-for-like replacement, even if in more modern materials. Again, it is helpful for you to have an ongoing plan for five or more years, including the whole of the premises. With a good plan, it may be possible to put the work out to tender and develop a relationship with a contractor for a period of time or cycle of work. Your LEA will be able to advise on the lifespan of equipment, and its periodic surveys of school premises, from which the asset management plans are developed, may be helpful.

Over time, the furniture, fittings and equipment get worn out and need replacement. This should rarely come as a surprise and can therefore be planned for. The headteacher (with the support of the senior management team and input from all of the staff) will usually maintain a schedule, room by room throughout the school, prioritised according to the condition of the items included and with indicative costings. This schedule should then be approved by the premises committee, so that the finance committee can identify the budgetary needs over the coming years.

With an effective plan, it may be possible to place orders in good time to take advantage of purchasing offers. It should certainly be feasible to avoid the inevitable 'peak period rush', which results in many schools not having their new furniture for the start of a new school year. As soon as your budget is set for the coming financial year you should discuss this with the headteacher and ask that orders be placed without delay. You may even be able to order further ahead if your finances permit. Your local authority may have a scheme for central purchasing, which you might find helpful.

Grounds

Grounds maintenance is of considerable importance as both the formal playing fields and the informal play areas need to be suitable for their purpose and any school gardens need to kept in good condition. You may wish to consider both the level of routine maintenance required and the availability of restorative work, should it become necessary following adverse weather or vandalism. You could find out whether your local authority offers a central contract for this work – if so, it is likely to be more cost-effective than organising your own and you may be relieved of the responsibility of monitoring it.

Reactive repairs

This term refers to repairs that are necessary as a result of accidental breakage or vandalism, or unexpected wear and tear. Your school will need minor repairs on an ongoing basis and you should make sure that the headteacher is given an annual budget to pay for such work, together with access to helpful contractors to undertake it. It's important for broken windows to be fixed, graffiti removed and damaged items repaired without delay because this gives a message that you care about your school and don't want to see it in poor condition. Children must be able to enjoy their school and feel pride in it. Effective security measures can often minimise the levels of vandalism.

Your local authority might have a scheme to which you can contribute each year, under which major repairs identified in the asset management plan are scheduled during (say) a three-year period. Such schemes often provide for the inclusion of some categories of reactive repairs, acting as a sort of insurance fund for unexpected eventualities.

Inevitably, you will find that your budget is limited and that you will be unable to carry out all of the work you would like, when you would like. You can draw together the elements of redecoration, refurbishment, furniture, fittings and equipment, grounds maintenance and reactive repairs as aspects of a single maintenance plan. This way you can keep control over what is happening, make the best use of available funds and resources and try to obtain best value for the school.

Improvement

Only the very newest buildings are likely to be entirely suitable for the present needs of a school and, like the majority of governing bodies, you will have in mind a number of things you would like to do to improve your facilities. Examples are wide ranging, but could include

- the total replacement of life-expired buildings
- the addition of extra classrooms
- major work such as new roofs
- structural changes, such as new doorways, toilets or access
- the installation of specialist cabling
- the purchase of ICT systems.

Improvement work is generally described as capital expenditure. This can be met from a number of sources, including

- devolved capital – an annual lump sum from the LEA given to your school on the basis of its size
- seed challenge capital – contributions from a lump sum allocated by the government to the LEA (schools must raise some of the funds to qualify and must bid for this support)
- school support grants – annual lump sums, allocated by the government according to the size of the school
- Standards Fund grants – a range of government grants, some of which might be used to support improvement projects (the individual grants, their defined purposes and the flexibility in the way they can be used, all change each year)
- special funds – such as grants for the provision of disabled access or facilities
- savings from the revenue budget – usually described as the school's balances
- borrowings from the LEA's loan scheme
- money raised by the school – by fundraising or sponsorship.

You may be able to fund some medium-sized developments, such as new roofs or additional classrooms, by a mixture of LEA and school capital resources. Significant contributions from the school may enable the LEA to prioritise the work involved.

Major developments are usually funded directly by the LEA, using funding for which it has made bids to the DfES or, in some cases, by approvals

An example school premises plan

The school premises plan should ideally form one section of the school development plan. It should serve as an overview document, summarising the key elements of the detailed working plan held by the headteacher.

	Item	Action required	Cost	Timing	Notes
Capital					
Developments	New rooms	Develop plan with LEA for two teaching rooms adjacent to A4/5	£140k from LEA	2004/5	LEA to seek funding Remember fixtures, fittings, furniture
Improvements	Main block roofing	LEA to arrange, out of term time	£85k from LEA	2003	In Asset Mgt Plan as category B2 item
	Boys' toilets in science block	LEA to arrange, out of term time; school to meet 50% of cost	£38k £19k from devolved capital	2004	In Asset Mgt Plan as category C2 item
	Disabled toilet	Adj. to above	£18k	2004	Bid from Access Fund
	Boiler	LEA to arrange, out of term time	£72k £10k from devolved capital	2004/5	In Asset Mgt Plan as category C2 item
Revenue					
Redecoration	School hall	Ongoing contract	£18k	2002	Devolved capital
	Dining room	Ongoing contract	£14k	2003	PTA fundraising Seed Challenge
	External	Ongoing contract	£23k	2003	Devolved capital
	Classrooms	New contract required	(est.) £120k	2004	Three-year contract
Refurbishment	Toilets in arts block		Redecorate	£8k	2002 Devolved capital
	ICT suite	Complete refurb.	£28k	2003	LEA loan over 3 years
Equipment	New tables	4 rooms	£6k	2003	Furnishing fund
		5 rooms	£8k	2004	Furnishing fund
	IT projector	Main hall	£3k	2003	Fundraising
	SmartBoards	Science rooms	£18k	???	Bid for funding
Grounds	Contract	Currently runs to 2003	(£14k pa)	2003	Consult LEA
Maintenance	Routine matters	Annual budget for headteacher	£16k	Ongoing	Annual review

for Public Private Partnerships or Private Finance Initiatives.

The LEA's asset management plan schedules the condition of school buildings and identifies all capital work that has been agreed with the governing body. The premises committee will wish to review this plan at least annually and consider whether any changes should be made, based upon new circumstances or needs. Because this is a long-term plan, linked to the school development plan, you can use it to allocate the school's own resources over future years. The work to be carried out can be planned well ahead, not only to fit into the annual timetable, but to make sure that the school's physical resources are stretched as little as possible.

In all cases, if you have effective liaison with the LEA and good working relationships with its officers you will earn maximum support for the school and, most importantly, for the headteacher in the management of the school while work is in hand.

Some capital projects involve little or no building work. An example might be the fitting out of a classroom for particular children, or the purchase of a range of ICT equipment. In such cases, your LEA may be able to offer purchasing advice or support.

See the example of a school premises plan opposite.

Catering

Governing bodies now have increasing responsibilities with regard to the provision of school meals and you might decide to allocate this aspect of your work to the premises committee. Your LEA must delegate the funding for meals to secondary schools, which can find that the issues relating to issuing sophisticated tenders, engaging contractors, monitoring service delivery, specialist health and safety and so on are quite complex. LEAs must also delegate funding to any primary school that seeks it, but you will need to think very carefully before taking such a decision, particularly about the management issues involved. It's likely that your headteacher won't welcome the additional workload involved.

You may decide that the best course of action is to enter into a contract negotiated by the local authority and then use the LEA's specialist staff to address any issues that arise. The school's responsibilities are then limited to the collection and banking of dinner money, the engagement and management of midday supervisors (needed whatever lunchtime facilities are in place) and the provision of a suitable space for dining. Under such arrangements the school is not responsible for any aspect of the kitchen or the staff who work in it.

Health and safety

Health and safety is a complex area in which many people have elements of responsibility, including the LEA (and possibly the foundation), the governing body, the headteacher, often one or more staff representatives, everyone who works in the school, everyone who hires the buildings or grounds out of school, and even the children themselves. Although LEAs have health and safety advisors, and schools have nominated health and safety officers, these individuals have a coordinating and supporting function and can't be expected to undertake full responsibility for health and safety issues themselves.

However, the wording in the *Roles of Governing Bodies and Head Teachers* (DfEE, 2000, p15) is absolutely clear. It states that, with regard to health and safety, it is the responsibility of the governing body 'to prepare a health and safety policy, carry out risk assessments and set up arrangements to manage health and safety in foundation and VA schools. In community and controlled schools this is the LEA's responsibility.' It's the responsibility of the headteacher 'to comply with the LEA's directions in community and VC schools. In VA and foundation schools to comply with governing body directions.'

The requirements differ, depending on the classification of school – effectively depending upon who employs the staff. Section 17 of *A Guide to the Law for School Governors* (DfES, 2001) deals with health, safety and welfare and sets out the responsibilities. The version for community schools suggests that you read and discuss the LEA's health and safety policy, and consider producing a school policy (your LEA may require you to do this).

It says that you should

- make sure that there are procedures for carrying out the LEA's policy
- decide whether you should have a health and safety committee
- implement procedures on issues such as accident reporting, health and safety inspections and staff training
- review these procedures regularly
- decide whether to have regular health and safety reports from the headteacher so that you can monitor safety

- take reasonable steps to make sure that the buildings, equipment and materials are safe and don't put people at risk
- review risk assessments
- make regular health and safety inspections
- bear in mind the LEA's policies and procedures when considering buying and maintaining equipment, operating laboratories and gymnasiums, and in arranging for non-structural repairs, cleaning and so on.

Your school has a wide range of policies, covering all sorts of subjects, eventualities and circumstances. Only a few of these are legal requirements – and a health and safety policy is one. It's a good idea for the premises committee to review your health and safety policy each year. Ask members to read both the current policy and Section 17 of *A Guide to the Law for School Governors* in advance of the meeting and to spend time thinking about whether the policy covers your responsibilities, whether it is clear to everyone concerned and whether it truly promotes and protects the health and safety of everyone associated with the school. A model health and safety policy is provided on pages 142–3.

Insurance

Insurance is an important issue for all schools and it is the responsibility of the governing body to ensure that it is addressed in an effective manner, to avoid undue risk and potential liability. Most local authorities or foundations, as the ultimate owners of the buildings, require that schools should be fully insured. In addition to the repair and maintenance schemes such as those outlined above, there tend to be four categories of insurance for schools.

1. **Contents** – insurance of the school's contents against common risks, such as theft. This may be undertaken directly by the school or, more commonly, through a bulk scheme organised by the local authority.
2. **Fixed assets** – insurance of the buildings themselves, together with fixed plant. This is most commonly undertaken through a local authority scheme, as individual cover based on individual risk, and tends to be considerably more expensive.
3. **Liability** – such matters as public liability, which are usually incorporated into a single policy with fixed assets.
4. **Staff absence** – you may want to try to minimise the risk of a high level of staff absence and the related costs of supply cover by contributing to some form of staff absence scheme, under which you pay a fixed contribution that meets all related costs. Your LEA probably runs such a scheme.

Contracts, purchasing and best value

Your local authority has standing orders relating to contracts, purchasing and tendering and the LEA scheme of delegation probably requires you to follow them, or to have some appropriate regulations of your own. You have to consider such regulations when you are entering into contracts for services or purchasing equipment.

The principles of 'best value' apply throughout local authority decision-making processes and, although they are not yet a legislative requirement for schools, many schemes of delegation do seek that they should be followed. They are in any case good practice, in that they provide effective guidance and support for contracts and other purchasing. As a governor – particularly if you are on the premises committee – you need to develop an understanding of best value. This is encapsulated in the 'four Cs' – challenge, compare, consult, compete. These may be summarised for schools as follows.

- **Challenge**, which ensures that questions are asked about the need for the product or service, its importance to the school and its place in the school's priorities. You may want to give consideration to the implications of different levels of service or quality of product.
- **Consult**, which involves asking the users of the product or service, to give them a voice in the decision-making. This may involve children, staff, parents or the wider community.
- **Compete**, which provides an opportunity for a wide range of suppliers to quote for the product or service, coupled with a fair judgement of both the price and the quality.
- **Compare**, which asks whether the product or service that has been used to date is the most appropriate, or whether other schools have reached more useful conclusions, or whether other providers might have alternative solutions.

The headteacher will be familiar with your LEA's procedures and the support it can offer in these matters. As a governor, you also need to be aware of such things. If you hold an office such as chair of the governing body or chair of the premises committee, then you need to take a special interest and satisfy yourself that the principles of best practice are being met.

Multiple use

The most valuable physical asset for any local authority is its school buildings and grounds – and yet they are in use for their core purpose for less than 20 per cent of the time. While it would be unreasonable to seek to use premises for 24 hours of every day, this general underutilisation is being widely addressed. The buildings belong to the community and yet, in so many cases, the community doesn't benefit from them in any capacity but that of a school. The same principles broadly apply to aided and foundation schools.

There are very many ways in which schools can be used out of hours, ranging from the educational to the purely commercial. These include

- before- and after-school clubs
- crèches and other childcare
- evening classes
- groups using ICT equipment
- play schemes and other holiday projects
- youth theatres and music groups
- local authority youth services
- conferences and staff training
- uniformed organisations such as Scouts and Guides
- senior citizens' clubs
- libraries, surgeries, village hall and parish council activities
- sports teams
- polling stations, public meetings
- commercial hirings for functions.

There are a number of considerations to bear in mind when determining a lettings policy and the related charges to be made.

Management

The management of lettings can be a time-consuming activity. It involves taking bookings, arranging for evaluation visits, agreeing specific terms, ensuring that the agreed facilities are available, ensuring that security facilities are in place, arranging additional cleaning and, finally, issuing invoices and collecting payments. In larger secondary schools there is usually a member of staff who is responsible for these duties – the level of use and the income generated justify this cost. However, in many primary schools this task falls upon an already stretched headteacher. In many cases the head also undertakes responsibility for access to the school's buildings out of hours, even though this might better be the responsibility of a caretaker or site manager.

Location

Appropriate spaces must be allocated for each letting. School halls are usually multi-purpose and can be laid out as needed, for example, for sports or larger meetings. However, consideration has to be given to any displays that are in place and any valuable equipment normally stored in the hall. Primary classrooms may not be suitable for many uses, owing to the small size of the tables and chairs, and the multitude of displays on the walls and other surfaces. The staffroom might be usable, subject to the approval of the staff themselves. Playing fields present fewer difficulties, so long as there are suitable changing rooms, and so long as the playing surfaces are not over-used. Some groups, such as uniformed organisations and play groups, need storage space for their equipment in order to function effectively and this can sometimes be difficult to provide.

Directed use

Legislation allows LEAs to have **directed use**, where they instruct schools to allow use of their premises for such activities as adult education, specifying the arrangements for access and the costs to be met. A number of LEAs still use this power, but most now feel it appropriate to negotiate lettings in the same way as any non-commercial user.

Income

What should your charges be for lettings? This is generally for the governing body to decide in that you should set out a policy and then allow the headteacher to implement it as they deem appropriate. The guiding principle is that the school must not subsidise outside users. The charges made must at least cover the costs incurred. You needn't have a single set of charges, however, and you might want to have some sort of differentiated scale, depending on

- the nature of the hirer – for example, a commercial letting might be charged a higher rate than a youth group
- the amount of space being used and the facilities and equipment required
- the staff costs involved for caretaking and additional cleaning
- reasonable contributions to heating, lighting and other overheads, and towards general wear and tear.

Income from lettings at community schools belongs to the LEA but financial delegation

A model lettings policy

Guiding principles

The school buildings and grounds are a community asset and every reasonable effort should be made to enable them to be used as much as possible. However, lettings for any purpose other than that of the school itself should be within the authority of the school, should not cause undue difficulty in the delivery of education, and should meet the general guidance laid out below.

Category of users

There are three distinct categories of letting.

1 **Self-managed** – activities that support the school or its children directly or are to the benefit of the school or the LEA. Examples would include peripatetic music lessons, parents' clubs, school nurse and dentist, staff training and LEA meetings.

2 **Community** – activities that are for the benefit of the wider community, possibly including children from the school, and are organised by non-commercial or charitable bodies. Examples would include before- and after-school clubs, crèches and other childcare, evening classes, play schemes and holiday projects, youth theatres and music groups, local authority youth services, uniformed organisations such as Scouts and Guides, and senior citizens' clubs.

3 **Commercial** – hirings by appropriate organisations of a commercial nature. Examples would include training companies, publishers' book sales and slimming clubs.

Charges for lettings

The charges for lettings will be reviewed from time to time, based on proposals from the headteacher.

1 **Self-managed** – there will be no charge for these activities, which will be regarded as 'internal' usage. Any modest costs for services such as heat or light will be met by the school.

2 **Community** – the school is not empowered to subsidise such activities from its own resources and a charge will be levied that meets the additional costs incurred by the school. This will include services (heat and light), staffing (additional caretaking and cleaning) and a modest contribution to wear and tear. There will not normally be an additional charge where school equipment is used. Where there are multiple lettings at the same time, the costs incurred will normally be shared between them.

3 **Commercial** – the charge for such lettings will be based on the community charge, together with a profit element. There will be an additional charge where school equipment is used. Where there are multiple lettings at the same time, the costs incurred will not normally be shared between them.

Management

The headteacher is responsible for the management of lettings and will, through the office staff, take bookings, ensure that bookings forms are fully completed, fix charges, arrange staffing and equipment, and collect the charges. The headteacher will determine whether lettings are appropriate and, where the head has concerns or wishes to decline a booking, they will consult with the chair of the premises committee, who is empowered to determine the issue on behalf of the governing body.

Some regular users may be provided with their own keys to the building, through a nominated individual, providing certain conditions can be met. These include the signing of an indemnity and the keyholders' register, and the undertaking of security training.

All hirers must be made aware of the school's policy on health and safety and, for all events where the public are to be admitted, appropriately qualified first-aiders must be present.

schemes probably allows the school to retain the income if you meet the costs involved. If you have a reasonable level of lettings, the school can earn a significant income, which can then be applied towards the costs of the school in any way you see fit. It may be added to the delegated funding, or accumulated for specific purposes, such as buying equipment.

For a model lettings policy, see opposite.

References

DfEE (2000) *Roles of Governing Bodies and Head Teachers*. London: DfEE.

DfES (2001) *A Guide to the Law for School Governors – Community Schools (Primary)*. London: DfES.

Election candidates have the right to use schools for public meetings, subject to availability, at normal charges. Returning Officers can require that appropriate buildings are used as polling stations, but schools may only claim the out-of-pocket expenses incurred.

There may be circumstances where the headteacher considers a potential letting unsuitable and, in such a case, they should usually review the matter with the chair of the premises committee or the appropriate officer at the LEA.

A model health and safety policy

Please note: this model is for community schools – different arrangements will apply in aided and foundation schools.

Guiding principles

Everyone who uses the school, its buildings and its grounds, whether pupils, staff, parents or visitors, have the right to be protected from health and safety hazards and for any incidents that do occur to be treated in an appropriate manner. In return, regular users should expect to be familiar with the school's health and safety policy and practices and to act in a responsible manner, to protect themselves and others.

It is the responsibility of the LEA to prepare a health and safety policy, carry out risk assessments and set up arrangements to manage health and safety. The LEA's statement of intent, health and safety guidance, monitoring procedures and accident reporting procedures have been adopted by the school and copies are to be held by the headteacher, all deputy headteachers, the school secretary, the caretaker and the chair of governors. All employees of the school are to be provided with a personal laminated copy of the Health and Safety Summary, which includes outline principles, accident procedures and the procedures for reporting concerns.

The governing body discharges its health and safety responsibilities through the premises committee.

The headteacher is the named person with overall daily responsibility for health and safety issues in the school. The head reports to the premises committee each term on any health and safety matters, including amendments to LEA policies or practices, risk assessments carried out and any incidents that have occurred.

The school has a nominated Health and Safety Officer and the teachers' unions have nominated a Health and Safety Representative – they have a coordinating and supporting function but do not undertake full responsibility for health and safety issues themselves.

Accidents

If an accident occurs to any person on school premises, it must be reported to the headteacher or, in their absence, to a deputy headteacher. They will determine whether there has been a reportable injury and act accordingly. Where circumstances are deemed to require it, the headteacher or deputy headteacher will call an ambulance and the member of staff witnessing the accident will be at hand to advise the ambulance personnel. No child will be taken to the hospital without a member of staff in attendance. All accidents, however minor, will be recorded in the accident book. The cause of any reportable accident will always be investigated by the headteacher or deputy headteacher. Accidents to pupils will be reported to parents. The headteacher will ensure that all reportable accidents and all bumps to the head will be notified directly, either by telephone or by hand-delivered letter.

First aid

The headteacher will ensure that sufficient members of staff receive first-aid training, including necessary refreshers. The list of trained first-aiders will be displayed on all notice boards, inside every classroom and workplace and at the school office. At no time may school be in session without sufficient first-aid trained staff being present and activities outside the school must either have a first-aider present or have immediate access to one. The school staff will not normally administer medicines, unless a written agreement has been drawn up with the parents or carers and medical advice has been taken.

Inspections and hazards

There are routine procedures for inspecting the premises. These involve the headteacher, the nominated Health and Safety Officer, the teachers' union Health and Safety Representative and, by invitation, the chair of the premises committee, conducting an annual tour of all parts of the school and grounds, to identify any risks or hazards. A checklist provided by the LEA is used to supplement the school's own schedules. Where any issues are identified, these will be reported upon and, on a termly basis, the same individuals will identify what action has been taken to resolve them.

Everyone in the school is responsible for identifying hazards. The headteacher, using their own experience and by reference to the LEA's health and safety advisor where appropriate, will assess any risk and determine the appropriate steps. If any hazard cannot be immediately removed, large warning notices will be displayed and appropriate staff notified.

Security

Children, staff and visitors must feel secure while on school premises and all reasonable steps will be taken to ensure that this is the case, without resorting to extreme measures. The school's security procedures are reviewed annually by the headteacher, the nominated Health and Safety Officer and the teachers' union's Health and Safety Representative. Any proposed changes to them are reported to the premises committee. A key principle is that, while children and staff should be able to move freely about the premises, visitors must be signed in and required to wear a security badge. Closed-circuit security cameras are in place and are monitored and there is control over vehicle movement on the site.

Fire precautions

Notices regarding the action to be taken in the event of fire will be displayed on all notice boards, inside every classroom and workplace and at the school office. All fire exits will be clearly marked and must be kept free of obstructions at all times. Practice evacuations will take place at least termly and staff will record the outcomes and any concerns. Inspections of fire safety equipment will be carried out regularly and there is a maintenance contract for all extinguishers and hoses.

Educational visits

Whenever educational visits take place the LEA procedures are followed and the necessary risk assessments are carried out. All members of staff planning or participating in such visits will receive a briefing in advance from the headteacher or deputy headteacher. Where appropriate, the LEA health and safety advisor is consulted about the visit.

Staff health and welfare

All staff have been issued with LEA guidance concerning stress and violence in the workplace and are personally informed of school procedures relating to health and welfare. Sickness reporting procedures have been advised to staff and they are aware that such absence is monitored. The school may make use of local authority personnel in matters concerning health and welfare. Any member of staff can approach the headteacher on any personal matter in complete confidence.

Contractors

Contractors working on the school premises must report to the office, where they will be provided with a copy of the school's guidance document. Any contractor not familiar with the school and not on the list of preferred contractors may be asked to sign a safe working undertaking.

Discover the Primary Leadership Collection

Primary Leadership Books

Primary Leadership No 46 Finance

ISBN 1 874050 66 X
£15.00

Primary Leadership No 47 School Improvement Planning

ISBN 1 874050 67 8
£15.00

Primary Leadership No 48 Environmental Issues

ISBN 1 874050 68 6
£15.00

Each book comes with a CD-Rom

Primary School Handbooks

The Governor's Handbook

The complete guide for the school governor.

ISBN 1 874050 54 6
£15.00
Additional copies £7.50

The Positive Behaviour Handbook

The complete guide for headteachers and staff for promoting positive behaviour throughout your school.

ISBN 1 874050 71 6
£15.00
Additional copies £7.50

Each book comes with a CD-Rom

The Solutions Series

Raising Additional Income

ISBN 1 874050 72 4
£5.00

Your Budget

ISBN 1 874050 73 2
£5.00

Financial Management

ISBN 1 874050 74 0
£5.00

In association with *www.capitaeducation.net*

Online Training

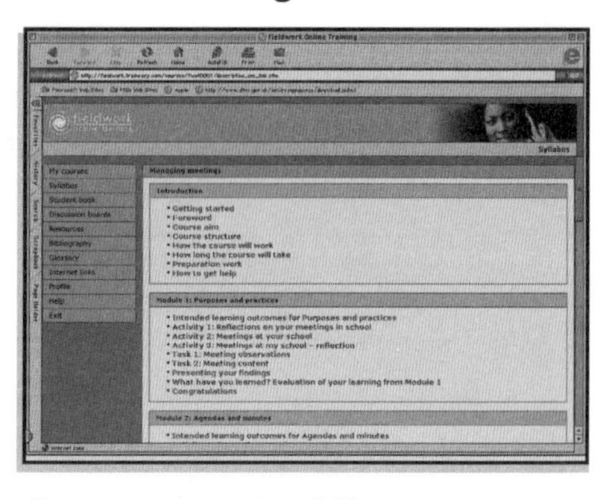

Two courses currently available

Managing School Finance

£60.00

School Self Evaluation for Governors

£60.00

Order Now

T: 0845 602 4337 F: 0845 602 4338

www.pfp-publishing.com

practical resources for school leadership **pfp**